THE
WORK
OF
THE
PASTOR

THE WORK OF THE PASTOR

VICTOR D. LEHMAN

JUDSON PRESS
Valley Forge, PA

THE WORK OF THE PASTOR

Unless otherwise indicated, Bible quotations in this volume are from the New Revised Standard Version of the Bible (NRSV), copyright ©1989 by the Division of Christian Education of the National Council of the Churches of Christ in the United States of America. Used by permission. All rights reserved.

As indicated, other Scriptures are quoted from THE MESSAGE, copyright ©1993, 1994, 1995. Used by permission of NavPress Publishing Group. The *Holy Bible,* New Living Translation (NLT), copyright ©1996. Used by permission of Tyndale House Publishers, Inc., Wheaton, IL 60189. All rights reserved. The New American Standard Bible, ©1960, 1962, 1963, 1968, 1971, 1972, 1973, 1975, 1977 by The Lockman Foundation. Used by permission. (NASB)

Library of Congress Cataloging-in-Publication Data

Lehman, Victor D.
    The work of the pastor / Victor D. Lehman.—1st ed.
        p. cm.
    Includes bibliographical references and index.
    ISBN 0-8170-1473-X (pbk. : alk. paper)
    1. Small churches. 2. Pastoral theology. I. Title.
    BV637.8.L44 2004
    253—dc22
                                                                    2004017261
Printed in the U.S.A.

10 09 08 07 06 05 04
10 9 8 7 6 5 4 3 2 1

This book is dedicated
as a tool
to aid pastors in
carrying out God's call.
Welcome to a journey of
lifelong learning.

CONTENTS

A Healthy Philosophy of Ministry

G OD'S SERVANT, PREACHER, TEACHER, COUNSELOR, EVANGEL-
ist, community example, office manager and office-
machine expert, volunteer coordinator, and general fix-it
(or clean-up) person—these are just some of the expectations
placed on pastors. Like a crowd of witnesses, these expectations
cry out to pastors, calling them to fulfill multiple and varied roles
in response to the needs of the church and community. Add to
these the often-muted voice of the pastor's personal roles of spouse,
parent, and child of aging parents and the challenging nature of life
as a pastor becomes clear. How does one person respond effectively to such an array of demands and expectations? How can one
finite person become, as the apostle Paul put it, "all things to all
people that [we] might by all means save some?" (1 Corinthians
9:22b). Or should a pastor even try? And how, in light of this host
of expectations, does one set reasonable limits and boundaries?

For the pastor, bombarded with expectations, a critical place to
begin is with a healthy personal philosophy of ministry. Now, some
may respond to this by thinking, "Not me. I don't need any philosophy," then run off to meet yet another expectation. Let me first
point out that those who respond this way may very well be head-
ed for burnout. Secondly, everyone has an operational philosophy,
whether or not it is thought-out or verbalized. In this case, it might
be characterized as "I'd rather burn out than rust out," and while
that could sound spiritual at initial hearing, it is not a very healthy
philosophy. God does not call us to either extreme. Such a philosophy sets a pastor up for the impossible task of meeting all expectations. Burn out or rust out; either way we are out—out of ministry and unable to serve God effectively. Ministry is a long-term

endeavor, so it is important to seek God's agenda, rather than any misguided extreme.

A helpful book for further study in finding God's agenda is Kirk Jones's book entitled *Rest in the Storm: Self-Care Strategies for Clergy and Other Caregivers*. Jones stresses finding a balance that avoids both the unrealistic expectations of congregations and the personal "self-violence" of overcommitting oneself. When assessing the real cost of pastoral caring, Jones's book helps the minister focus on what can be changed by asking three important questions:

- To what extent do caregivers experience self-inflicted, unnecessary suffering?
- How much of the healer's hurting may be attributed … to unhealthy beliefs and behaviors regarding the essential relationships between personhood, vocation, recreation, and rest?
- Are there alternative understandings and strategies that will allow clergy … to minister and serve more frequently out of spiritual, psychological, emotional, and physical abundance, not scarcity? (Jones, p. xi)

Unique to Jones's book is the development of the picture of Christ, who found his way to the back of the boat and fell asleep, finding rest even in the middle of a storm. Jones encourages pastors to learn to do this as well.

Risky philosophies that pastors often fall into include the one-person-show, the never-say-no, and the humble-smugness philosophies.

One-person-show pastors need to do everything in order for things to be perfect and to meet personal expectations, and therefore simply cannot ask for help. Notice that the primary focus here is on the self. The agenda is to meet personal, often perfectionist, expectations with the hope that this will please God. Perhaps this attitude is apparent in King Saul, when he grew impatient waiting for Samuel to arrive and so he went ahead with the altar sacrifice that the law permitted only a priest to offer (1 Samuel 13:8-14). To Saul's horror, he discovered that God is not pleased with the act of sacrifice in itself, but desires a humble and contrite heart. Carrying out a personal agenda, rather than God's agenda, is costly.

Never-say-no pastors assume that since they are God's representatives and servant leaders, they are not at liberty to refuse any request that comes to them. It is quite easy for pastors to try to play the role of savior or martyr: to rush to the rescue at every call or to feel responsible to "fix" situations. But we are pastors, not saviors. Christ is the Savior. No pastor can save anyone. Only God can. We can offer support, prayer, guidance, and the ministry of presence, and then trust God to be at work in the lives of others—saving within and "fixing" on the outside.

Some pastors approach ministry as if they think, "Ministry is for God and I am the one trained and qualified for ministry, so then only I can carry out the job with excellence (as defined by my view of God's expectations)." Do you notice a little "humble smugness" here? There's a sense that God cannot use lay people as well as those who are seminary trained. Yet doesn't God look for willingness, sometimes at the expense of excellence? Think of reluctant Moses or fearful Gideon or bumbling Peter. Throughout the Scriptures, we see God using ordinary people—complete with stumbles and bumbles—who were faithful. Excellence is a worthy goal, but spirit-empowered giftedness serves the even more worthy goal of faithful service for all. Christ's whole body needs to be properly involved in service to God, and wise pastors allow room for the efforts of all members of that body.

While the three philosophies outlined above may be appealing in some ways, each is a time bomb waiting to go off. Each has more to do with personal ego and the desire to do good in order to look good rather than because of genuine service. And none supports a healthy approach to ministry or faithfulness to God. In contrast, consider these three, healthier understandings of ministry: I am

God's servant first; my primary job is to coach others in their service to God; and living a Christ-like life is my priority.

I am *God's* servant first.

Opportunities to minister abound. Since the pastor is first *God's* servant, this approach begins with the question "What is *God* calling me to do?" Prayer becomes a major component in living out this philosophy with the primary goal being to please God. There is recognition that God does not call the pastor to meet all needs and expectations. There is an understanding that the pastor is not called to make everyone happy and a realization that happiness is a personal choice, so no one can make another happy. This philosophy can help us as pastors to winnow needs and expectations down to actual ministry so that God can use us more effectively. There are always choices to be made, and we need God's wisdom to make those choices well. The assumption within this philosophy is that we need to seek God's agenda and, in turn, God will provide the time and energy for us to fulfill that agenda.

My primary job is to coach others in their service to God.

This philosophy recognizes that all disciples have spiritual gifts that need to be used in service to God. Ministry becomes a team effort and pastors do not see themselves in ministry alone. Even during those times when we may feel like Elijah, hiding in a cave and wanting to die because we are convinced that we are the *only* ones left still faithful to God (see 1 Kings 19), this understanding assures us that we are not the only faithful ones left. Rather, we know that God is building a team, called "church," and God wants us to help build that team. This approach encourages us to focus on what will help the team grow and bring glory to God. It reflects the thinking found in Rick Warren's *The Purpose Driven Life* that it's not about us. The pastor becomes a team player and a player coach, effectively working with others to serve the Lord.

Living a Christ-like life is my priority.
The focus here is on "being" first, and then on "doing." Too often these are reversed with what we *do* as pastors overriding who we *are*. In this priority of living a Christ-like life, the emphasis is on being God's person first and allowing activity to flow out of the person God is making us into. The primary goal is to seek strength from God to live a Christ-like life, anticipating that living such a lifestyle will encourage others toward that same goal.

These three understandings of ministry are offered as beginning points. They are not mutually exclusive, nor are they comprehensive. It is important for pastors to develop philosophies of ministry that flow from their own gifts, abilities, and relationships with God. One approach is to develop a philosophy around key Scripture passages. I have found 2 Timothy 2:15 helpful in focusing my personal philosophy of ministry: "Do your best to present yourself to God as one approved by him, a worker who has no need to be ashamed, rightly explaining the word of truth."

This verse serves to remind me that God is the first one I need to please and that my primary task is to handle God's Word accurately. This means that preparation for sermons and teaching receives a very high priority. This is a pattern I find attested to by Christ's first disciples when they instructed the people in the Jerusalem church to select people to wait on tables, so that they could devote themselves to prayer and serving the Word (Acts 6:2). The charge to pastors is to present the Good News of Jesus Christ in the most powerful way possible. To be able to do this, we must ground ourselves in the Scriptures so that we can present to others ways of living them out in daily life. Both interpretation and application of the Word require accuracy.

In further developing my own personal philosophy of ministry, I have found Ephesians 4:11-16 to be very instructive on matters of working with the body of believers. I approach this within the categories of limitation, purpose, goal, and process.

Limitation: The use of the word "some" in Ephesians 4:11 makes it clear that not one person can carry out all roles. "The gifts [Christ] gave were that some would be apostles, some prophets, some evangelists, some pastors and teacher …" This picture of a variety of gifts being given to different people is helpful for setting limits to the pastor's job.

Purpose: The sentence continues with an emphasis on empowering others rather than trying to handle all aspects of ministry: "to equip the saints for the work of ministry, for building up the body of Christ …" (Ephesians 4:12).

Goal: The goal of this gifting and empowering is the same for pastor and people. That goal is maturity: "until all of us come to the unity of the faith and of the knowledge of the Son of God, to maturity, to the measure of the full stature of Christ" (Ephesians 4:13).

Process: The process requires full participation. Within the body of believers, each person has a part to play, a role to fulfill, and each needs to be working properly in order for the whole body to be healthy. One part of the body is not designed to do all the work alone—not even the pastor.

> But speaking the truth in love, we must grow up in every way into him who is the head, into Christ, from whom the whole body, joined and knit together by every ligament with which it is equipped, as each part is working properly, promotes the body's growth in building itself up in love. (Ephesians 4:15-16)

Based on Ephesians 4:11-16, my personal philosophy of ministry can be summarized as follows: As pastor, I am a player-coach, who first gleans and lives out God's truth in order to teach that truth, so that others may accurately live it and teach it. Depending on the size of the church I serve, my primary team is my staff or my key lay leaders, who in turn will work closely with the larger team, the church as a whole.

A pastor's philosophy of life and ministry will greatly impact how the work of pastoral ministry is carried out. Developing a healthy philosophy and allowing it to guide ministry and ministry's many choices is essential. A healthy philosophy encompasses both being and doing. In other words, it helps in the effort to balance who we are and how we function. The effort to find that balance must be ongoing if pastors are going to have a solid basis from which to approach this great challenge called "pastoral ministry."

What follows are tools that will help build a healthy philosophy of ministry, a philosophy which will then serve as a solid basis from which to carry out the work of the pastor. This book addresses both being and doing, and while the bulk of it focuses on the "doing" part of pastoral ministry, the first part is dedicated to the person of the pastor or the "being" part of ministry. This is intended to emphasize the importance of who we *are* as the foundation of what we *do* as pastors. Within Part One, we will look together at pastoral identity, highlighting calling and giftedness, then move into a discussion of developing our potential as pastors with discussions of personal spirituality, personality traits, self-care, and ministerial ethics.

Part Two then focuses on a wide range of topics related to the doing part of serving as a pastor. This includes discussions on worship, pastoral care, conflict management, team ministry, administration, and outside affiliations. Part Two closes with a look at considerations related to transitions in pastoral ministry.

The purpose of this book is to help pastors, especially those in churches of fewer than two hundred members, decipher their roles in light of personal gifts, the changing context of ministry, and the unique culture of a particular church. This material will be especially helpful to new pastors and seminary students across denominations. While the solo or senior pastoral role (as distinct from specialists such as music ministers or youth directors) is the primary focus here, direction is given for working with volunteers or staff in specialized ministry positions. It is my hope that this book will be a practical tool for pastors, and so I have included a list of recommended resources at the end of each chapter and offered some useful appendices at the end of the book.

May this book be helpful in pointing you toward effective ministry for our gracious God.

Recommended Resources

Jones, Kirk Byron. *Rest in the Storm: Self-Care Strategies for Clergy and Other Caregivers.* Valley Forge, Pa.: Judson Press, 2001.

Warren, Rick. *The Purpose Driven Life.* Grand Rapids, Mich.: Zondervan, 2002.

PART ONE

The Person of
the Pastor

CHAPTER 1

Identifying What We Are Given

“WHAT YOU ARE DOING SPEAKS SO LOUDLY, I CAN'T HEAR what you are saying.” “Do as I say, not as I do.” These familiar sayings highlight a potential problem for pastors. Who we are directly impacts the effectiveness of our ministry. If we fail to “walk the talk,” as it is commonly put, then it is not likely that our people will strive to be Christ-like either. Additionally, people desire genuineness in the person they call “pastor.” Genuineness means a real person, not a perfect person (with whom they cannot identify), but a person who sincerely cares for them and has their best interests in mind. A genuine person demonstrates humility by being a good listener, expresses honest concern for the opinions of others, and provides sound feedback. In chapters one and two, we will focus on the person of the pastor and consider several components of “being real.” We will begin in this chapter by exploring the package that each one of us is, considering the notions of calling and giftedness, and then move on to look at the ongoing work of developing our potential through managing personal spirituality, personality traits, self-care, and ministerial ethics.

Each of us comes to ministry as a “package deal.” Part of the package is intrinsic and includes things such as gender, racial-ethnic identity, and intelligence level. Another part of the package is extrinsic, such as marital status and choices about bivocational ministry. All of these factors impact how we serve in pastoral ministry and how we are received. It is beyond the purview of this book to deal with each and every one of these variables; however, don't overlook their significance. I encourage all pastors to explore these topics further. Good resources abound on a wide range of related topics. Examples include *Church Administration in the Black Perspective* by Floyd Massey Jr. and Samuel B. McKinney, which deals with factors specific to the African American congregation; *All I Need to Know about Ministry I Learned from Fly Fishing* by Myrlene L. J. Hamilton, in which the author honestly shares the struggles of being a female pastor in a male-dominated vocation and deals with issues faced by dual clergy couples; and *The Bivocational Pastor: Two Jobs, One Ministry* by Dennis Bickers, which provides insight from his personal experiences in bivocational ministry. It is important to invest the time to find resources that speak to your specific situation. Start with catalogs from your favorite publishers, or pursue specific topics on the Internet or at your local library. Seminary librarians can be very informative, as can professional colleagues who have "packages" similar to your own.

For the purposes of this book, we will be looking at two qualities that are common to all pastors, irrespective of individual distinctions. These are calling and giftedness.

Calling

Pastoral ministry is very hard work. The people served often find it easier to criticize than to commend. Then too, concrete results in ministry are hard to see. There are many motivations for entering pastoral ministry. It is important to ask ourselves hard questions, such as, Do I have the assurance that I have a call to ministry from God? Or, am I a pastor because it was what my parents wanted, what my friends all expected of me, or because I thought it meant working only one day a week? There is only one motivation that can keep us going through the normal struggles that come with this territory: that is a calling from God. At times during pastoral ministry, our call is the only thing to which we can cling to keep from giving up. In tough times, I have found myself turning to God with pleas such as, "God, you called me to be a pastor. You placed me in this particular ministry setting. You need to carry me through." Assurance of God's call is an essential and solid foundation for ministry.

What does such a call look like? Basically it is a deep sense in the very depth of our beings that we need to be in ministry. It is a strong conviction that no other job will bring us fulfillment and meaning in life. One pastor, when asked how we can *know* we are called by God into ministry, responded, "When you can't do anything else." He did not mean that ministry is for those who cannot succeed in the "real world," but that ministry provides the fulfillment of the soul's yearning in a way that no other job can. So if you are a person who is very unsure of your call to ministry, it would be wise to try other pursuits first, and then if your soul finds no rest, intensely seek from God whether ministry is the answer for you.

An important aspect in identifying a call to ministry is to realize that the call may well be progressive. In my own life, I felt called to full-time Christian ministry during my first year at Bible college. Since then the specifics of my call have ranged from youth ministry to family ministry to Christian education to the pastorate to seminary teaching to writing in practical theology and then back to pastoral ministry. In each case, the call to full-time ministry was constant, but the application varied. On the other hand, I have friends who have been called to a particular ministry, such as youth ministry or music ministry, and have remained there throughout their vocations. The call of God, then, is dynamic, and each of us must be faithful to both the general and the specific direction God gives us. Viewing a call to ministry this way is more appropriate than approaching different levels of ministry as stepping stones to more prestigious positions.

A helpful manual for guidance through the process of assessing call is Alice Cullinan's book *Sorting It Out: Discerning God's Call to Ministry.* Cullinan seeks to come alongside Christians of all ages and with varying levels of experience who sense God's calling, and help them assess the authenticity of the call and whether it is to lay or ordained ministry. Robert Schnase's *Testing and Reclaiming Your Call to Ministry* is a good resource for persons already in ministry and struggling with the decision to remain there. Time spent affirming and reaffirming personal call to ministry is time well spent.

Giftedness

It is very helpful for pastors to take a course on spiritual gifts or at least to do some self-testing to determine spiritual gifts. The Houts Modified Gifts Inventory, which is found in C. Peter Wagner's *Finding Your Spiritual Gifts*, is a twelve-page, self-test booklet designed to reveal a specific cluster of giftedness that, in turn, points to an appropriate type of ministry. For example, a combination of preaching, teaching, and administration works well for a lead pastor position in an established church. The gifts of evangelism, discernment, and mercy go well with church planting, outreach, and evangelism. A primary and single gift of helps indicates that pastoral ministry may not be the best place to serve. So, discovering our giftedness not only helps confirm call, but it also guides us to an appropriate church setting and area of specialty. A tool for more extensive personal assessment is *Networking: Equipping Those Who Are Seeking to Serve* by Bruce L. Bugbee. The newest version of this resource includes a participant's guide coauthored with Don Cousins and Bill Hybels.

One single test, of course, does not necessarily give the final word. Throughout active ministry, certain gifts will be affirmed and reaffirmed by people as they experience our use of them. What repeatedly comes back can be taken as a solid measure of our giftedness. Diagnostic testing services, then, are a helpful starting point and also a base line against which to measure this feedback.

Recommended Resources

Bickers, Dennis. *The Bivocational Pastor: Two Jobs, One Ministry*. Kansas City, MO: Beacon Hill Press, 2002. Available at www.BeaconHillBooks.com.

Bugbee, Bruce L. *Networking: Equipping Those Who Are Seeking to Serve* (1989) and distributed by The Charles E. Fuller Institute (P.O. Box 91990, Pasadena, CA 91109-1990, or call 1-800-999-9578). Look for the newest version, which includes a participant's guide (see below).

————, Don Cousins, and Bill Hybels. *Network: The Right People. . . In the Right Places. . . For the Right Reasons*. Grand Rapids, Mich.: Zondervan Publishing House, 1994.

Cullinan, Alice R. *Sorting It Out: Discerning God's Call to Ministry*. Valley Forge, Pa.: Judson Press, 1999.

Hamilton, Myrlene L. J. *All I Need to Know about Ministry I Learned from Fly Fishing*. Valley Forge, Pa.: Judson Press, 2001.

Massey, Floyd, Jr., and Samuel B. McKinney. *Church Administration in the Black Perspective, Revised edition*. Valley Forge, Pa.: Judson Press, 2003.

Schnase, Robert C. *Testing and Reclaiming Your Call to Ministry*. Nashville, Tenn.: Abingdon Press, 1991.

Wagner, C. Peter. *Finding Your Spiritual Gifts*. A twelve-page test booklet to determine our spiritual gifts is available from Christian Book Distributors. Call 800-CHRISTIAN or order online at www.christianbook.com.

CHAPTER 2

Developing Our Potential

THE "PACKAGE" A PASTOR HAS BEEN GIVEN IS ONLY AS GOOD as its use and development. If a person never responds to God's call or fails to use his or her personal giftedness, both the person and God's kingdom lose. But if what we are given by God is nurtured toward maturity, ministry begins. Potential must be developed and managed in order for ministry to be effective. In this chapter, we will explore developing potential in the areas of spirituality, personality traits, self-care, and ministerial ethics with an eye toward enhancing effectiveness in ministry.

Personal Spirituality

Pastors need a specific plan for personal spiritual growth. Study for sermon preparation alone is not enough. The personal devotional study of God's Word touches us at a different level. It is during personal devotional study that we look at Scripture to see what *we* need to learn, what *we* need to change with God's help, and what *we* need to confess. While it may be easier to identify what others need to hear from a given passage or how others should change, Scripture exhorts us to begin with ourselves. Paul's warning reminds us to run the race well ourselves, "lest possibly, after I have preached to others, I myself should be disqualified" (1 Corinthians 9:27*b*, NAS).

It can be helpful to experiment with methods of personal study; however, it is important to practice discipline and stick with the process. Choose a devotional *plan* that works for you and be regular about the process, even if you need to change your *method* of devotional study. For example, try reading through the Bible in an unfamiliar translation at a comfortable pace, or select a single verse and stay with it for as long as it continues to feed you, even if it lasts a year or two. For example, Psalm 4:1 offers many levels of meaning for one seeking to plumb its depth.

The key is to do what keeps God's Word fresh for you personally. In addition to regular Bible study, prayer time that includes quietly listening to God and practicing the spiritual disciplines are helpful in the essential effort to grow personally in the spiritual realm. A very practical guide for practicing the spiritual disciplines, such as prayer, meditation, solitude, etc., is *Celebration of Discipline* by Richard Foster. I have even used it as a source for a sermon series, to teach our congregation the spiritual disciplines.

Personality Traits

Along with giftedness, an honest assessment of personal strengths and weaknesses is a helpful basis from which to approach ministry, especially as pastors seek to develop their leadership styles. One philosophy is for pastors to lead from their strengths and essentially cover up their weaknesses, so strengths are honed to fine skills until they overshadow weaknesses. Another perspective considers God's "upside down Kingdom" and encourages leading from weakness, for then and only then will pastors depend on God and allow God to make them strong (2 Corinthians 12:9-10). Henri Nouwen, in his book *The Wounded Healer,* discusses a similar idea of how a pastor can speak relevantly from personal suffering to a world full of suffering.

In reality, pastors end up leading from both strengths and weaknesses, according to the needs of the moment. Ministry is a stretching experience and often pushes us outside our comfort zones. If and when ministry pushes us outside our ability zones (e.g. calling on a non-singer to sing), then it is time to invite someone else to address that need. It is simply very practical to know before we try something whether we are coming at it from strength or weakness. In some cases, we may need a team member to come alongside us in order to be able to carry out the needed ministry, as in the case with tongue-tied Moses, who needed eloquent Aaron. Honest assessment of human limitations goes a long way in helping pastors be both genuine and effective.

What personal characteristics make for a good pastor? Actually, it is amazing whom God can use. A brief survey of Bible characters or church history quickly reveals God's ability and willingness to use people with a wide range of strengths and weaknesses. For example, as Moses and Gideon both learned, God's call to leadership receives priority over human weakness. However, certain character traits do lend themselves to effective ministry. Based on the recommendations for elders in 1 Timothy 3:1-7, I suggest that God looks for the following qualities in leaders: spirituality; a gentle, teachable spirit; high integrity at home and in the community; self-control in all conduct, including eating and drinking; a balance of imagination and common sense; and a sense of humor. Each of these traits is highly valuable for effective ministry.

Self-Care

We live in an era characterized by lack of restraint. In fact, society today "preaches" that we deserve to have all our needs and wants met immediately. A biblical idea—more specifically a fruit of the Spirit—called self-control is no longer prized, but self-indulgence is. As a result, obesity tops the list of dangerous health risks for the American people. Unfortunately, a large number of pastors fall into this excess. In addition, sexual misconduct on the part of pastors tears apart many churches. Scott Larson reports in *Rev.* magazine that "one in three pastors will have an extramarital affair during his or her ministry career" (p. 53). This is unacceptable. The excesses need to stop. By God's grace, self-control needs to rule the day.

Self-restraint is a critical aspect of self-care. As Margaret Kornfeld suggests in *Cultivating Wholeness*, since pastors are counselors in congregations, they need advice about how to care for their own needs as they navigate the complex and demanding tasks of pastoral ministry. It is essential, then, for the pastor to exercise good patterns of self-care, of holistic care, since "there is growing public acknowledgment, supported by research, that the body and the inner experiences of mind, emotion and spirit, are inextricably related" (Kornfeld, p. 6). Good self-care is very helpful in avoiding excesses and indiscretions.

Care for the body is also an important part of ministry. Just as the pastor cares for the church building as well as for the people, so too do pastors need to care for their personal temples of the Holy Spirit. Nutritious meals, regular exercise, appropriate rest and relaxation, even good hygiene and proper clothing are part of the job of being a good minister, because each of these areas directly impacts who we are and how we reflect Christ. This means that pastors do not need to feel guilty for taking much-needed breaks or for making the time to exercise regularly. These are part of the job God has called us to do.

I struggle with trying to exercise at least three times a week for 30 minutes each time, and some weeks I am more successful than others. The key is not to give up. I view each new week as an opportunity to try again. It is amazing how much stress is reduced by regular exercise. Equally amazing is how fast tension builds up to become pain in my body when I neglect exercise. Something else that really helps me reduce stress is to read a chapter of a good book throughout the day. I personally find this better than a coffee break, although keeping fluids up is also an important part of self-care. For me, drinking water while reading works well. I enjoy inspirational fiction. Just a ten-minute break reading something that totally captivates my attention gives me energy to resume my work. It is important to find what works and what provides a brief moment to stop and smell the roses. It is also important to be careful not to become consumed by the break. Books that just cannot be put down can easily have this effect. Again, self-restraint is needed.

How a pastor dresses not only reflects on one's own person, but also on the church. Clothing does not need to be elaborate, but it should be appropriate to the community context. While some churches may be too sensitive, there is some merit to a concern such as, "Our pastor dresses so shabbily it makes it look like we don't pay enough." In some situations the church may in fact not pay enough, but it is better to find a direct way to ask for a raise. Appearance also reflects on the God we serve. Moderation and cleanliness are good guidelines to follow.

Another very important aspect of self-care is being part of a support and accountability group. Many denominations sponsor support groups, which are sometimes referred to as "cluster groups." My own denomination, American Baptist Churches U.S.A., considers support groups to be so important that they have received a grant to help fund what they are calling "Covenant Groups." As the name implies, the participants covenant to be together regularly, perhaps every four to six weeks, to share and study together. It is important to check into what is available in your area and through your denomination.

The group I am currently part of is wonderfully supportive. We are studying *Cultivating Wholeness: A Guide to Care and Counseling in Faith Communities* by Margaret Kornfeld to help us in the whole area of holistic care. We are learning how to facilitate inner healing, adapt to constant change, and form genuine community, so that we can in turn bring healing and wholeness to our congregations.

For those who prefer a stronger theological focus, a comparable resource is *Self-Care: A Theology of Personal Empowerment and Spiritual Healing* by Ray S. Anderson. This book also focuses on inner healing that empowers future ministry.

Ministerial Ethics

A carefully maintained, high standard of integrity and ministerial ethics is especially important today and goes hand in hand with good self-care. Limits and boundaries need to be defined early on to head off potential problems. Our world needs more examples like Job, Noah, and Daniel, who, in the midst of incredible evil, lived lives of faith and integrity.

Personal integrity includes being true to God, to loved-ones, and to ourselves. It consists of everything from avoiding the appearance of evil in moral conduct to paying bills before moving out of town. Many denominations have pastors sign a code of ethics as part of the ordination process or as part of accepting a pastoral position. The code of ethics can also provide a benchmark for periodic evaluation of personal conduct. (A sample ministerial code of ethics is provided in Appendix A.)

The person of the pastor is the greatest resource anyone brings to ministry. As Rick Warren put it in *The Purpose Driven Life*, we are "human beings" first and then "human doings" (p. 177). Who we are will have the greatest impact on what we can do in ministry. This reality demands that we take seriously the responsibility to take the best care possible of the person of the pastor.

Recommended Resources

American Baptist Covenant Groups. For more information, visit www.ministerscouncil.com.

Anderson, Ray S. *Self-Care: A Theology of Personal Empowerment and Spiritual Healing.* Wheaton, Ill.: Victor Books, 1995.

Foster, Richard J. *Celebration of Discipline: The Path to Spiritual Growth.* 20th Anniversary Edition. San Francisco, Calif.: Harper Collins Publishers, 1998.

Kornfeld, Margaret Zipse. *Cultivating Wholeness: A Guide to Care and Counseling in Faith Communities*. For the Blanton-Peale Institute. New York, N.Y.: Continnum International Publishing Group, 2001.

Larson, Scott. "Factual Accountability: When Moral Failure Hits Close to Home." In *Rev.* magazine, July/August, 2001. (Available at P.O. Box 469102, Escondido, CA 92046-9688, or online at www.OnlineRev.com.)

Lehman, Victor D. *The Pastor's Guide to Weddings and Funerals*. Valley Forge, Pa.: Judson Press, 2001.

McKinney, Lora-Ellen. *View from the Pew: What Preachers Can Learn from Church Members*. Valley Forge, Pa: Judson Press, 2004.

Nouwen, Henri. *The Wounded Healer: Ministry in Contemporary Society*. New York, N.Y.: Doubleday, 1990.

Trull, Joe E., and James E. Carter. *Ministerial Ethics: Being a Good Minister in a Not-So-Good World*. Nashville, Tenn.: Broadman and Holman, 1993.

Warren, Rick. *The Purpose Driven Life*. Grand Rapids, Mich.: Zondervan, 2002.

PART TWO

The Work of the Pastor

CHAPTER 3

Worship and Serving the Word

THE BEST GIFT A PASTOR CAN BRING TO MINISTRY IS A WHOLE self, growing and maturing in Christ. Too often ministry is short circuited because of personal limitations, such as poor self-esteem. This is evidenced in ministers who give up too easily, who regularly exhibit defensiveness and a fragile ego, or who readily overreact in pride or anger. In Part One, we explored the "being" aspects of pastoral ministry as the essential foundation for effectiveness. In Part Two, we turn our attention to the "doing" aspects of pastoral ministry by considering the various expectations facing pastors, with primary focus on churches of fewer than two hundred members that are served by solo pastors. The reader is invited to draw implications for larger settings or specialized ministries. While the goal of this resource is to be neutral in matters of gender and race, adaptations may need to be made to accommodate the suggestions to specific situations.

For purposes of discussion, the work of the pastor has been divided into six areas. This chapter begins with a look at the pastor and worship. Those who genuinely seek to worship our great and awesome God are called to worship "in spirit and in truth" (John 4:23). While most Christians accept this goal, the questions remain of how to get there and what true worship looks like.

Determining worship style in any congregation is a challenge. Worship, defined as the experience of actually encountering God, touches emotions deeply. As a result, people speak passionately when describing their worship preferences. Seldom is there complete agreement on how worship should be conducted. Whether pastors are dealing with associate ministers, lay worship leaders, or worship committees, the challenge of shaping good intentions into effective worship for the whole church is a constant.

A good way to begin is by listening to see what the people in a given church's culture need in order to meet and interact with God. Starting with listening and slowly moving the church forward is far better than bringing in the latest ideas or insisting on immediate changes. At the same time, however, it is important to keep the big picture in mind. Beyond the local church's desires and expectations, there appears to be an ebb and flow in worship style preferences within the larger Christian community. This factor is especially important when there is a desire to attract new people to the church.

Choices about worship style often mean making tradeoffs. For example, a popular option for worship is to offer two services with different styles: a contemporary worship experience and a more traditional one. This division is helpful where opportunity and resources allow. Some churches choose to have two services with the same worship style to prevent competition between the services. This option is limiting, however, since a wider range of needs can be met by offering different styles of worship.

For the church that can offer only one option, a blended worship experience is popular. A blended service involves using both contemporary choruses and traditional hymns. This works especially well if the worship leader is sensitive to the needs of those who are present. Speeding up traditional hymns a little and slowing down praise choruses somewhat can help temper resistance. In the church I currently serve, the people enjoy an upbeat tempo, but they don't appreciate singing the same verse of a chorus too many times, even when the song is written that way. Another variation is to divide up each month by having one traditional service (perhaps on Communion Sunday), two blended services, and one contemporary service. Other options are also possible, of course, and sometimes it is necessary to experiment to find what best fits a particular church.

Pastors do well to keep current with worship resources so they can present a variety of options. This can be done by attending workshops or simply by reading. It is advisable to discuss various options with the worship committee or even the church council or board prior to "experimentation," especially if the service structure is set. This keeps pastors from unnecessarily setting themselves up for criticism. Pre-approval is also important to the health of the church, because of the strong feelings that surround worship choices and the risk of conflict inherent in changing worship style. This conflict can even become strong enough to split a church. Brad Berglund's *Reinventing Sunday: Breakthrough Ideas for Transforming Worship* offers additional ideas for working with worship changes.

One practical suggestion for creating quality worship services is to keep a log of hymns, choruses, and other service elements that are used. A sample log is provided in Appendix B of this book. A suggested guide is to not repeat music for a three-month period, unless the congregation is learning a new song. This process helps to insure use of a wider range of materials and encourages more comprehensive use of hymnals and songbooks. Many of us have thirty or so favorites we find it easy to fall back on, especially when in a hurry. A rich resource of music is available to the church and drawing from its variety can greatly enrich worship.

Sermon Preparation and Preaching

Sermon preparation and preaching will rightly consume the majority of a pastor's time. The disciple's admonition in Acts 6:1-4 is still appropriate for today:

> Now during those days, when the disciples were increasing in number, the Hellenists complained against the Hebrews because their widows were being neglected in the daily distribution of food. And the twelve called together the whole

community of the disciples and said, "It is not right that we should neglect the word of God in order to wait on tables. Therefore, friends, select from among yourselves seven men of good standing, full of the Spirit and of wisdom, whom we may appoint to this task, while we, for our part, will devote ourselves to prayer and to serving the word."

Too often pastors are caught up in "serving tables" while the ministry of the Word is neglected. The pastor's primary tasks are prayer and serving the Word, and so these must be high priorities. Other carefully selected team members, whether lay or ordained, are gifted by God to carry out other areas of service. Pastors need to find those people and empower them to do their tasks. Care must be taken, however, to heed the warning of Ezekiel 34 and not to go to the opposite extreme. There the prophet chastens the shepherds for being so busy feeding themselves that they neglect the needs of the sheep. Pastors need to be examples of service, so it is important to find an appropriate balance.

As for specific ideas for sermon preparation, much depends on personal style. Some pastors enjoy doing all their research and sermon preparation on the Internet. There is an ever-increasing number of resources to draw on for this endeavor, and you will find some examples in the resource list for this chapter. For pastors who prefer hard copy to cyberspace, there continue to be some very helpful subscription-based preaching resources, and some of these are mentioned in the resource list also.

Whatever the personal choice for research, there is still no replacement for personally wrestling with the text. In my experience, God's sense of humor has been revealed as interactions have been sent my way during the week that directly fit the theme on which I am planning to preach. So pastors who plan to speak about patience may expect all kinds of trials during the week. This phenomenon helps preachers to live God's Word first, and then to speak it. Pastors need to avoid being caught as the brunt of the old story shared by Myrlene Hamilton, in which an old Pennsylvania Dutchman referred to road signs as "ministers," and when asked to explain why, said, "Because they point the way, but they don't go there themselves!" (*All I Need to Know…*, p. 37).

When pastors allow God to make the text real in their own lives first, it adds to the credibility of preaching and makes it possible for heart and head to work together in preparing the message of God for God's people. If a sermon is not coming together, a good approach is to ponder, "What is this text saying to me; what is going on in my life right now that this text is speaking to?" Studying commentaries and other resources on the text can then help confirm and develop seeds generated by personal reflection.

Pastors do not need to wait until a text is perfectly applied in their own lives before preaching it. It is powerful for pastors to share their own struggles and cutting edges as they try to live out God's Word. Some listeners will better identify with this humanness, which reflects their own struggles, than with messages that suggest we have it "all together."

One of the greatest challenges in sermon preparation is choosing what text or topic to use each Sunday. It is helpful for pastors to come up with systems that are longer-ranging than merely going Sunday to Sunday. The stress of choosing anew each week is more than needs to be borne. Ideas for a longer-range system include: preaching a series, such as on characters of the Bible; dedicating a period of Sundays to a book of the Bible; doing a topical study, such as on the fruit of the Spirit or names of Jesus; addressing a series of issues, such as social concerns; or working with key verses in Scripture. I am currently working with monthly themes during which I preach four sermons on a given topic. For example, in a series on forgiveness, I have offered four sermons entitled "Can I Forgive God?," "Can I Forgive Myself?," "Can I Forgive Others?," and "Can I Forgive and Forget?" Sermon planning is limited only by the imagination. Be sure to allow the Holy Spirit to quicken yours.

Another way to facilitate long-range preaching is to spend half a day or more in a personal retreat to seek God's guidance on what to preach on in the coming year. I find it helpful to spend some time in the sanctuary at the beginning of a sermon planning retreat. I visualize the members of the congregation by where they usually sit and ask God what their needs are. After jotting down a list of the needs of the people God has called me to serve, I make a list of possible sermons or sermon series that would speak to those needs. For example, if several families are going through crises, I might plan a series of sermons on coping with difficulties. Or, if I become aware that a number of people are dominated by fear, I will opt to address that issue. Next, I sit down with a calendar and plot out the year, observing special Sundays that have their own themes, and scheduling my topics and series in the remaining spaces. Of course the entire process is sustained throughout by prayer. This is why a retreat setting, in which I am away from the telephone and other interruptions, works so well.

Another approach to sermon planning is to choose a lectionary that is appropriate for your congregation. Some denominations approve a lectionary annually or have developed a lectionary that rotates in a multiyear cycle. Lectionaries provide Bible readings for each Sunday and provide a good beginning place. The listed passages can be reviewed and selected according to what seems relevant to the congregation's needs. Lectionaries are also helpful for highlighting special days, such as Unity Sunday in January or Worldwide Communion Sunday in October.

Sermon length varies according to the church's tradition and the pastor's style. Although there is no hard-and-fast rule, a sermon needs to be long enough to convey God's message properly, yet not so long that it puts listeners to sleep. Twenty to thirty minutes is usually appropriate. Much longer than that and the preacher risks becoming redundant. Much less and the people may not have sufficient opportunity to connect with what God desires to communicate through the preacher. Some articulate people can say everything that needs to be said in fourteen minutes. These are, of course, only guidelines. Some African American preachers typically can hold an audience for an hour or more. They make very artistic use of repetition. And some preachers can find a way to be boring in ten minutes or less. The point is that a message should be as long as it needs to be to accomplish its purpose, but no longer. Here, personal giftedness and the style and expectations of the church are important considerations. It is likely, however, that people are more likely to stand up and call you blessed if the sermon is too short rather than too long.

Preaching style will vary according to personal ability and preferences. While some pastors prefer the freedom of preaching without notes, others prefer taking a full manuscript into the pulpit. Other options include preparing an outline, using a highlighted manuscript, or reading a narrative. Pastors need to do what frees them up to speak God's Word confidently and clearly.

Many congregations appreciate pastors varying their preaching styles. For example, my latest venture involves writing a three-part historical fiction work that offers inspiration by putting scriptural principles into everyday living. My goal is to inspire people to live out the Bible in their daily lives. Their attention to the story is incredible, and the ongoing nature of the story encourages regular attendance. I have known pastors who prefer to preach three short sermons separated by music, drama, Scripture, or prayer in the course of the worship service, rather than one longer sermon. In one case, I employed the youth group to dramatize my illustrations during a sermon. Boy, that kept the attention of observers—and of participants!

Teaching

In addition to preaching, "serving the Word" involves teaching. While some pastors teach from the pulpit and others use Bible study as just another opportunity to preach, both avenues of serving God's Word are effective. They work best, however, when they provide distinct variety for the congregation. Churches that still have Sunday evening services or Wednesday Bible studies provide additional opportunities for using each gift—preaching and teaching.

Preaching tends to be one-way communication, although the pastor can be aware of and learn to interpret the body language of listeners, and in some church traditions (most notably in the black church) the congregation is an active participant in "talking back." In contrast with even the most interactive preaching traditions, teaching allows for more direct interaction and discussion between the teacher and learners. Teaching the Bible provides the opportunity to hear how people understand texts and to explore together the connection between Scripture and daily living. It is important to resist any temptation to approach teaching as modified preaching. This often happens when lecture is the primary teaching method. At its best, teaching draws people out and enables them to interact with the texts themselves. In this approach, the Bible comes to life for all involved and learning is interactive. Even though extra preparation is required, teaching a weekly Sunday school class in a preferred age group provides a powerful ministry opportunity. It allows for the development of mentoring relationships between the pastor and class members.

Other areas of ministry commonly call on the pastor to step into the role of teacher. These include premarital counseling sessions and baptism, confirmation, and new member classes. The spiritual gift of teaching is a valuable asset for any pastor, and it is worth developing teaching skills. If teaching, however, is simply not your gift, it is important to identify those who are skilled teachers, lay or clergy, and team up with them to provide a strong teaching ministry.

In my ministry, I think my teaching has done more to help people grow spiritually than has my preaching, simply because teaching enables me to help the students wrestle with the text personally, where it applies to them specifically. Teaching allows me to proceed at the pace of the students' assimilation, and answer their questions along the way. Preaching is more confined by time and application to a larger audience.

Seasons of the Church Year and Other Special Days

There are many special occasions to celebrate regularly in the church, each of which enriches our worship experience. Some come by way of the Christian calendar, which is optional in its usage but which can provide helpful ideas for sermon topics.

For example, the four Sundays prior to Christmas are called Advent. Advent is a season dedicated to preparation to celebrate the coming of the Christ Child. Pastors may want to do some research on Advent to prepare for the season and plan a special sermon series that reflects on the Christmas story characters and their responses to the promise of Christ's birth. Such Advent characters might include Elizabeth, Zechariah, Mary, Joseph, and Jesus himself. Such a sermon series would help God's people keep their focus on Christ's coming during the hectic pre-Christmas season.

Lent, which is also a season of preparation, includes the five Sundays prior to Palm Sunday and provides a framework for focusing on God's deliverance to us through the sacrifice of Jesus on the cross. This is wonderful preparation for the celebration of Easter Sunday. And, celebrating the ministry of the Holy Spirit during the season of Pentecost provides another focus to enrich your weekly worship services.

The regular calendar lists other special days that lend themselves to specific sermon topics. These include Mother's Day, Father's Day, Maundy Thursday, Good Friday, Labor Day, Remembrance Day, Christmas Day, and New Year's Day. In addition to special days, special events in the church also warrant topical sermons. One challenge that pastors may want to embrace is to come up with different emphases for each Communion service. For example, for a church that participates in Communion each month, twelve different sermons focused on Communion could be offered. This would make Communion central to the service, rather than something that is tacked on at the end. Suggested Communion topics include: Christ's choice of elements; what it cost Jesus to pay for our forgiveness; the celebration of "until he comes"; and how to be worthy to participate at the Lord's table.

Child dedications or baptisms are another precious opportunity to touch lives in worship. Whether the request comes from a couple or a single parent, it is important to honor the desire to dedicate or baptize a child. Whenever possible, it is a good idea to involve several generations in the special ceremony by offering choices of who will participate. Services can be designed to involve siblings, grandparents, or godparents in addition to the parents. Offering the parents a variety of Scripture readings and of vows from which to choose will make the event more meaningful. Some samples are provided in Appendix C of this book. It is important to keep in mind and to make it clear to the parents that the dedication or baptism of a child is also, and very importantly, a dedication of the parents. The ceremony highlights their intention to raise the child to know and love God. A parent who does not have a commitment to God may not be able to honestly make this commitment. Pastors need to work with each situation and guide parents to choose vows they can honestly make. In some cases, simply offering a blessing of the child, as Jesus did (see Matthew 10:13-16) may be more appropriate than a full dedication or baptismal service. Spending time with the parents in planning the ceremony is great pastoral ministry. It also gives the opportunity for the child or children to become comfortable with the pastor and for the pastor to become confident holding the child.

Believer's baptism and confirmation are significant events in the worship life of the church because they are the opportunity for participants to declare publicly their personal faith. For those who practice baptism of believers by immersion, the process provides a powerful symbol of dying to self (being lowered into the water), being dead to self and sin (buried under the water), and rising to new life in Christ (coming up out of the water) (see Romans 6:1-11).

It is crucial for anyone who is new to this procedure to practice baptizing on a volunteer before the service. The process involves the baptismal candidate bending his or her knees as the pastor lays them back into the water. The pastor also bends his or her knees to avoid strain on the back. For a large person, the help of a staff member, deacon, or family member might be needed. A family member may also be helpful for a candidate who is afraid of the water, and having a spouse present can be especially nice. Some people have a tendency to float and may not easily go fully under the water. It is advised to simply proceed with a smooth motion and not to worry if all the hairs on the person's head do not get completely wet.

There are a variety of ways to hold people for immersion, and pastors need to experiment to find a style that is comfortable. I prefer having the person interlace his or her fingers like in prayer. I hold one of the clasped hands at the wrist and between the palms. That way the person can squeeze his or her hands together on mine, getting a greater sense of security. My other arm goes across the shoulders at a height that is good for me to lower the person into the water. Some pastors prefer to place a washcloth over the individual's face before putting them under. I find this practice awkward to do and think it might feel smothering to the person. For anyone who fears water up the nose, however, this approach is helpful.

Other practical considerations for baptism by immersion include having the baptistery filled (hoping, of course there are no leaks—I've been there), warming the water to a comfortable temperature, and checking on special attire. Hip waders help reduce the risk of slipping and speed up changing time for a quicker return to the sanctuary. When planning the service, it helps to plan for someone to lead singing between each baptism, to give people time to come in and out of the baptistery. Finally, baptismal candidates should be advised to wear solid colored clothing for modesty, even when baptismal gowns are used, and they should be given a walk-through of the service ahead of time, so they feel comfortable.

Weddings

The invitation to be a part of a couple's wedding can stir up mixed feelings in pastors. On the one hand, a wedding is exciting for the couple and it can be an honor to be invited to lead this sacred ceremony. Likewise, this special time provides a unique opportunity for discipling, especially through premarital counseling that is focused on how to build a God-centered marriage.

On the other hand, weddings add a great deal of additional work to a pastor's busy schedule. Both the ceremony and the premarital counseling sessions deserve to be done well. In addition to the time commitment, pastors may also have ethical issues surrounding certain weddings. These are often issues that need to be dealt with delicately. For example, if one member of the couple is a Christian and the other is not, some pastors may consider 2 Corinthians 6:14 a prohibition against officiating at the marriage ceremony. Others may resist marriages that appear to be for convenience. My earlier book, *The Pastor's Guide to Weddings and Funerals*, addresses these and eight other ethical issues related to weddings.

The primary goal of a Christian wedding is for it be worshipful, and this fact must guide the wedding planning. A good ceremony fully honors marriage as an institution of God, whereby couples commit themselves to one another for life. Taking the ceremony flippantly, as something that is just read from a book, or with an attitude of "let's just get it over," is a sacrilege.

A good wedding is also joyful and therein lies the balance. It is easy for pastors to become so consumed with conducting everything correctly and solemnly that the joyfulness of the occasion is lost. I remember looking at the wedding pictures of a friend's daughter, and in every single one, the beautiful bride was solemn and unsmiling. When I asked why this was so, I was told that the pastor had so stressed the seriousness of their commitment throughout the wedding service, that the couple could not break the mood to laugh or even smile. How sad! It is important to allow joy to fill the service as well. This will also help minimize nervousness for all involved.

A good wedding depends on good preparation. While pastors need to accept couples as they are, premarital counseling goes a long way in equipping and orienting a couple to married life. It is standard to spend six one-hour sessions with a couple, covering a variety of topics. Allowing couples to select among a range of topics will make the process relevant to them and encourages continuation of the premarital preparation process. Suggested topics include communication, acceptance and self-esteem, involving God in the marriage, roles and expectations, and dealing with conflict. These and other practical ideas easily form a list of some twelve ideas from which the couple can choose six, or if the situation allows, all the topics.

Personality testing can show how well potential partners know each other and highlight areas of potential conflict. Several tests have been developed specifically for premarital preparation and some suggestions are included in the resource list at the end of this chapter. It is important for pastors to keep up-to-date by reading in the area of premarital and marital counseling. In circumstances where pastors do not feel comfortable handling premarital counseling, a colleague in ministry, counseling center, or an organization that offers premarital retreats can be called on. Personal contact with reputed specialists helps insure they are, in fact, trustworthy counselors.

Funerals

One of the most critical times for important pastoral care is when a death occurs. Being with the bereaved and offering comfort takes first priority. The pastor's presence is far more important in these moments than are the words that are spoken. As representatives of God, pastors offer the one thing that can help even in the midst of intense grief: that is God's love.

During times of loss, family members will often feel numb and things may seem chaotic, so it is valuable to have a worksheet on hand to help with funeral planning. The worksheet should provide a basic format that can be developed to suit the family's desires. A sample funeral packet can be found in *The Pastor's Guide to Weddings and Funerals*. It is also very important to be fully apprised ahead of time of local burial and funeral customs and to have that information reflected in the funeral worksheet. Questions to consider include: Is it customary to have a prayer service as well as a funeral? How do the two differ? What will the funeral home do and what will the pastor arrange?

A funeral service has a dual focus that needs to guide what pastors plan to say. The goal of a funeral is to respectfully remember the deceased while ministering to the living. To facilitate appropriate remembrance, the service may be life-based (especially when there is much in the deceased's life to celebrate), theme-based (focused on one aspect of the deceased's life or on one of God's characteristics), or gospel-based (dealing with basic salvation as the need of all people). Creativity is needed to highlight personal aspects of the deceased's life. Developing a tribute to the person that is drawn from the family's memories serves as a powerful way to personalize any funeral.

To facilitate ministering to the bereaved, it is vital to keep in mind that they are the ones who are still able to make choices and life changes in response to what is said at the funeral; the deceased no longer has needs. The critical question is how to appropriately and ethically build on the fact that death causes people to reflect on life and what comes after life. The gospel message of hope and salvation is for the living, so in addition to offering comfort, the focus needs to be on the choices they still face. People often need encouragement to express their grief and may depend on the pastor for help in making good choices for themselves even as they say a final farewell to a loved one. Pastors need to seek God's guidance to find the balance in offering comfort and in faithfully presenting the gospel of love.

Recommended Resources
BOOKS

Berglund, Brad. *Reinventing Sunday: Breakthrough Ideas for Transforming Worship.* Valley Forge, Pa.: Judson Press, 2001.

Hamilton, Myrlene L. J. *All I Need to Know about Ministry I Learned from Fly Fishing.* Valley Forge, Pa.: Judson Press, 2001

Lehman, Victor D. *The Pastor's Guide to Weddings and Funerals.* Valley Forge, Pa.: Judson Press, 2001.

Litchfield, Hugh. *Visualizing the Sermon: A Guide to Preaching Without Notes.* Self-published, 1996. Available through the bookstore at North American Baptist Seminary in Sioux Falls, SD.

McMickle, Marvin A. *Before We Say I Do: 7 Steps to a Healthy Marriage.* Valley Forge, Pa.: Judson Press, 2003.

LECTIONARIES

Revised Common Lectionary. For a Revised Common Lectionary that is adapted to Baptist life see www.abc-usa.org.

PREACHING HELPS

Pulpit Helps, a ministry of AMG International, 800-251-7206. (A phone call will often result in a free copy to peruse.)

Pulpit Resource, by Logos Productions Inc., 6160 Carmen Avenue East, Inner Grove Heights, MN 55076-4422, 1-800-328-0200. (Particularly helpful if you follow the Revised Common Lectionary.)

www.PreachingToday.com. (Now also available on Compact Disc from *Christianity Today,* 800-806-7796, offer KE3GE72, fee charged.)

SermonCentral.com, a ministry of Campus Crusade. (Many resources are offered free.)

www.HomileticsOnline.com (Rights are purchased with the magazine.)

PREMARITAL/MARITAL COUNSELING

Premarriage Awareness Inventory, Logos Productions Inc., 6160 Carmen Avenue, Inner Grove Heights, MN 55076-9910.

PREPARE and ENRICH. PREPARE is a testing inventory for premarital counseling and *ENRICH* is one for married couples. The latest inventories, materials, and training sessions available can be accessed at www.lifeinnovations.com.

Taylor Johnson Temperament Analysis process, Psychological Publications Inc., 5300 Hollywood Blvd., Los Angeles, CA 90027, or call 800-345-8378 for latest updates.

CHAPTER 4

Pastoral Care

DYNAMIC LEADERSHIP, VISIONARY PURPOSE, AND A SEEKER-sensitive focus all have their place in pastoral ministry, but what pastors really need to focus on as a solid base of ministry is shepherding the flock out of a sense of love. What do good shepherds do for the flocks that have been designated by God to be under their care? According to Jesus, ultimately the "good shepherd lays down his life for the sheep" (John 10:11, NLT). When not fulfilling this extreme calling, what are a pastor's other shepherding tasks?

Pastors tend the injured, regularly check on the condition of the sheep, and direct the flock, as individuals and as a group, to good pastures and safe waters. In this chapter, we will consider six areas of pastoral care that are common in pastoral ministry: crisis care, visitation, pastoral counseling, ministering to "extra-grace-required" individuals, helping abuse victims, and intervening with suicide risks. Then we will take a look at the importance of setting boundaries.

Crisis Care

The care and feeding of God's flock, as entrusted to pastors, is an awesome undertaking. Consider the weight of being responsible for the spiritual well-being of a whole group of people—not only to feed them weekly on God's Word, but also to be there when crises occur. Only God's love, shining through us, can accomplish so great a task. Therefore, it is essential to ask God often to fill us with great love for our people. A helpful book that develops the concept of learning to love the ones we lead is *They Call Me Pastor* by H. B. London Jr. and Neil Wiseman.

Since we live in a very depersonalized world, where people are hesitant to help others who are struggling, the members of the church flock need more than ever to feel that they are cared for and that their burden is not theirs to carry alone. They need more than ever to know that the pastor and church will do as Paul urges in Galatians 6:2: "Share each other's troubles and problems, and in this way obey the law of Christ" (NLT).

Crisis care involves standing with people in grief. As mentioned in the previous chapter, when the grief is caused by the death of a loved one, it demands top priority. Pastors do well to go immediately, if at all possible, to families touched by the death of a loved one to offer support and strength. Often people will need to replay the story of the death repeatedly, so pastors need to allow them to tell it as often as necessary. If pastors are fortunate enough to be present when death comes, part of the task becomes helping the surviving parties say good-bye.

Pastoral support is especially needed today, when life can be sustained artificially and tough decisions have to be made regarding life support. The role here is to help the family work through the decision and to support them in their choice, while being careful not to make the decision for them. It is also crucial to let the family make such a decision in their own time and not pressure any decisions before they are ready. A pastor's own view of death will come into play here along with the view the family holds. If these views differ, we may *gently* explain our view, but listen to theirs as well and leave the final decision between God and them. In other words, when leading is appropriate, do it by gentle influence and under God's guidance, seeking the appropriate response for the particular situation in which we walk with others through the valley of the shadow of death.

Crisis care is also needed when other significant losses occur, such as a miscarriage, a separation or divorce, a financial setback, or loss of employment. In some ways these situations are more volatile than a death. Usually when a death occurs, pastoral care is welcomed. In other losses there can be so much anger about the loss that the individual may not be able to receive pastoral care. Gracious support is needed in such a case and can take the form of offering help and issuing an open invitation, but gently backing away if met with resistance until God gives the sense that help should be offered again. Sensitivity to the Holy Spirit is essential here, for often a hurting person will not approach a pastor or will give only veiled signs of readiness to accept pastoral care. Gentle, persistent invitations will insure that pastors do not neglect the need for pastoral care or allow people to fall between the cracks. It is also valuable to approach both parties in a marriage dispute, listening to both sides of the story, so as not to be used as "collateral" for one side against the other.

It is important to remember that the pastor's task is not to rush in and "fix" every crisis, but rather to be God's presence in the situation, representing our God of infinite resources and healing.

Visitation

Visitation is a challenging and rapidly changing area of caring for the flock. While it is somewhat generational, there is increasing hesitation on the part of some church people to welcome pastors into their homes for formal visits. While at one time a common goal of pastors was to visit every member at least once a year, current privacy concerns have brought this goal into question. While members still need a personal touch from the pastor, many may no longer expect home visits. This is where pastors need to be creative and adapt pastoral care to the needs and openness of the each parishioner. While much of the older generation, particularly those in nursing homes, love visits, others may prefer phone or e-mail contact. All three of these forms of visitation are legitimate pastoral care, and some may require pastors to adjust to them. For example, praying with someone over the telephone may feel strange at first, but it can be a very effective form of pastoral care.

Hospital visitation has also changed over time. HIPPA regulations require explicit permission from patients to notify pastors of their status. This privacy issue is often directly affected by the trust level between parishioner and pastor. So, while some people are uncomfortable even to know that the pastor has discovered that they are in the hospital, many parishioners still appreciate a pastoral visit during their hospital recovery and a prayer prior to surgery or other significant procedure. Sensitivity to the desire of the patient is essential here, and the hospital staff (including, but not limited to the chaplain) can be a great help. If a visit to a hospital room is clearly unappreciated, a simple apology and graceful departure are in order. Mistakes will happen, but it is best to err in going and not being wanted, than not going and being needed by the patient.

Knowing the flock's desires and expectations, then, is essential for effective visitation. To learn who prefers what type of visitation, simply (and gently) ask what they would appreciate and try to accommodate their comfort zones. Mistakes will probably happen, but genuine concern can cover a multitude of faux pas.

Counseling

There are several levels on which a pastor is sought for counseling, including premarital, marital, family, and individual counseling. Premarital counseling is often the most delightful. Here pastors are usually working with a relatively healthy situation, with people who are growing in their love for each other and who desire to build a solid foundation for their future together. While some pastors may feel that little of what they teach during premarital counseling is heard because couples are so "ideal" in their new love, this time can be essential for building a solid relationship between the pastor and the couple. This relationship, in turn, provides a link so that when marital problems arise, the couple has a trusted counselor to turn to for help. This can be true even with couples who are not solidly connected with the church; therefore insisting on premarital counseling for all couples does build a solid basis for future ministry. Arranging for premarital counseling to be a church policy will reinforce the pastor's position. (For further ideas of topics for premarital counseling, see pages 27–29.)

Marriage counseling can be more challenging for pastors, because couples tend to develop destructive habits over time and these patterns cannot be quickly changed. Pastors are on the front lines of relationship checkups and can often see unhealthy patterns developing within couples. It is important to let people know that there are others ways to relate and to offer help when people are ready for it. Good listening and mediating skills are essential, as is the skill of asking appropriate questions. Jesus was a master at using this approach in a variety of situations with questions such as, "Do you wish to be made well?" and "Why do you call me good?" (John 5:6; Matthew 19:17). In addition to listening and questioning, pastors also need to be able to teach basic relationship and communication skills, similar to what is taught during premarital counseling.

Pastors are not therapists, however. Thus we need to know our limits and be careful not to go beyond personal expertise. A good rule is to set a limit of three to six sessions and then move to referral to a good counseling center. This means that pastors need to explore what counseling services are available in the area and build relationships with good counselors. Pastors may even consider taking a referred couple to meet the counselor in order to help establish that initial link and increase chances of follow-through by the couple. Care must also be taken not to turn vulnerable people over to those who will mishandle their situations. While there is a lot of good counseling out there, bad advice also exists, even to the point of extremes such as "What you need to add spark to your marriage is to have an affair outside of it."

When it comes to counseling individuals, effectiveness greatly depends on the giftedness and training of a given pastor. While opportunity will abound for simply being a good pastor by caring and listening, counseling interactions require taking simple precautions. For example, care must be taken in one-on-one counseling with the opposite sex. Simple common sense and appropriateness, rather than paranoia, go a long way. Jesus counseled women alone, but in a public place (e.g. the woman at the well). Even so, the encounter with the woman at the well was destined to raise some eyebrows. Still, Jesus gave the woman's need priority over the risk of negative speculation. Much pastoral counseling will be spontaneous as it occurs in a moment at the grocery store, a "chance" meeting (a.k.a., divine appointment) on the street, or in a brief visit in the church office. The potential for suspicion or even inappropriate behavior grows when a pastor repeatedly sees the same person in a private setting, so it is wise to minimize the emotional intensity of such encounters by leaving a door open to an outer office or by meeting in a public place. If a relationship becomes uncomfortable or inappropriate, it is time to refer. Care must be taken by pastors not to be seduced by the lure of being the only one who can help.

Similarly, it is important to avoid the trap of being the rescuer or savior. Jesus already has that job taken. When I find myself moved by a person's infatuation with my caring, when I am tempted to rescue an individual from dire circumstances, or when I begin to feel that I am the only one who can "save" someone, I know that I need to end the counseling relationship. Pastors cannot fix other people's situations. We need to trust God, give God the credit for any help we are able to offer, and recognize that God works through others also. Again, knowing when to refer to another counselor is critical. Whenever a counselee becomes dependent on a pastor, the relationship has become unhealthy and it is time to involve others. A helpful academic resource that touches on all aspects of pastoral counseling is *Pastoral Counseling* by Barry K. Estadt. A resource that seeks to help pastors deal effectively with the perils of ministry, such as sexual misconduct and burnout, is *A Time for Healing: Overcoming the Perils of Ministry* by Jody Seymour.

Ministering to "Extra-Grace-Required" Individuals

An "extra-grace-required" (EGR) individual is one who lives in constant crisis and continually looks to the church or pastor to "bail them out." Some EGR people have continual physical or material needs—such as transportation, health, and financial challenges; others have strong emotional and psychological needs. The person who *must* dominate every conversation has a need to be heard, because most likely they are not being heard elsewhere. The couple that turns every meeting they attend into a therapy session for themselves have deep needs. Most churches have at least one such person, but when a congregation has many such people, it can be a tremendous challenge for the pastor, making pastor burnout a significant risk.

Here is the tension. As a general rule, people are more important than things. However, when the "thing" is sermon preparation and the third call comes from the same person, now asking the pastor to meet yet another need, the priority changes. Now we are dealing with a "serving tables" issue, as discussed in chapter two of this book—remember the situation faced by the disciples in Acts 6:1-4?

When wrestling with this tension, a helpful question for pastors to ask themselves is, "Is meeting this need a high priority for me, as the pastor (e.g. death in the congregation), or is this need something that someone else in the church could handle equally well or better than the pastor (e.g. car trouble)?"

One key to helping EGR people and ministering to them as we should, since they are a part of the church, is to spread the load around. Put in place a team of people who are willing to help out with tasks such as rides to the grocery store, automobile repair, and listening to or praying with the person. Rely on that team as often as necessary, when the load becomes heavy or when you need time to focus energy elsewhere. But, delegate the responsibility with love and clear communication so that the needy person does not feel "dumped" or the volunteer, "dumped on." The pastor does not need to do it all on a regular basis, just a reasonable share, enough to be an example of willingness to help even with mundane tasks.

As pastors, we need to try to love such people—and help our congregation to love them—into greater wholeness. It is God's people who are to be known for their love to one another, not just pastors who are to be known by their love for parishioners. A classic book for training lay people to be caring toward struggling individuals is *Love, Acceptance and Forgiveness: Equipping the Church to be Truly Christian in a Non-Christian World* by Jerry Cook.

A practical resource for helping lay people in assisting with general pastoral care is *A Pastor in Every Pew: Equipping Laity for Pastoral Care* by Leroy Howe. This helpful book provides a theoretical framework for teaching how to do quality pastoral care, and it includes a training manual for use in a small-group or class setting. The manual is geared toward equipping church leaders to develop pastoral care ministries that make a lasting difference in the lives of others.

It is also OK at times to simply say "No" to EGR people. They are usually very resourceful and will find other avenues to having their needs met. Encourage them to take personal responsibility for their needs as often as possible. And, keep in mind that another responsibility of pastors is to set necessary boundaries in relationship with EGR people—for ourselves and for our team. Such boundaries are critical if larger ministry is going to happen. (More about boundaries later in this chapter; see page 43–44.)

Helping Abuse Victims

Two of the most difficult counseling situations pastors can face involve abusive situations and suicidal parishioners, both of which appear to be increasing in occurrence. In responding to either of these situations, allow me to underscore the importance of networking with professionals who specialize in these areas. A team approach is critical for dealing with these difficult, life-threatening, and also potentially litigious situations.

In cases of abuse, the victim may feel safe to report their traumatic experience first to the pastor, putting the minister in the position to initiate help for the victim. When this painful revelation happens, keep in mind these recommendations from a specialist who works with teenagers:

> Be prepared. Believe their reports. Assure them that you will help them to take appropriate action to stop the abuse and you will help them deal with their feelings about it. Encourage the [victim] to report the assault or abuse to a sexual assault agency. This specialized assistance can be invaluable. (*Fortune,* p. 13)

The key is to treat each allegation seriously, no matter what the age of the victim, and to draw in professional help. Since the pastor is seldom an expert in this area, it is also helpful to develop a sexual abuse policy for the church prior to a situation actually arising. In fact, many insurance companies are requiring such a written policy as part of continuing to insure the church and staff. My current church and I are working through this process right now. When we are done, the policy will include a step by step response format for allegations made, and key workers, including pastoral staff, will be required to have had a criminal background check done, all in accordance with insurance requirements. Our insurance company also recommends that a church lawyer be on the response team to help avoid future litigation.

Of course, not all victims will come forward with allegations or requests for intervention. So, in addition to developing a policy for dealing with such allegations, pastors should become familiar with signs of abuse. Being alert to recurring bruises and injuries and noting behaviors that may indicate sexual abuse, such as excessively sexual dress or flirtation, can help pastors identify abusive situations. When abuse is suspected, pastors are legally bound to report the situation to Social Services. It is important, therefore, for pastors to build a network of social workers and other helpers, such as the police, who can be called on when help is needed. Even when others are called in, pastors can stand with parishioners in a loving way and provide a safe environment for victims until proper help is available. When it is permitted by Social Services, a child who is removed from his or her home may feel less afraid if taken into care by a church family rather than by strangers.

This resource is not intended to be comprehensive in its treatment of the subject, so pastors are strongly urged to participate in workshops or engage in careful study of resources, such as *Sexual Abuse in Christian Homes and Churches* by Carolyn H. Heggen, *Pastoral Care for Survivors of Family Abuse* by James Leehan, and *Sexual Abuse Prevention: A Study for Teenagers* from the Center for the Prevention of Sexual and Domestic Violence.

Intervening with Suicide Risks

In situations where someone indicates that he or she is suicidal, intervention is essential. Experts tell us that the more specific a person is about how they will end their life, the closer they are to carrying it out. Specialists usually ask, Have you thought of ending your life? How often do you think about it? What method would you use? The more affirmative and detailed the response, the more urgently intervention is needed. In working with possibly suicidal parishioners, it is suggested that any innuendoes about suicide be brought out into the open and they be asked directly if they are having thoughts of hurting themselves. And, of course, all responses need to be taken seriously.

In some rare situations, pastors may want to enter cautiously into a pact with a parishioner in which that person promises to call, day or night, the next time suicidal feelings arise. In some cases, this agreement will be enough to deter suicide. It becomes a rope of hope to cling to. However, realize the seriousness of such a commitment for the pastor. Are we truly available to a parishioner at any given moment? Where available, a suicide counselor would better fill this role.

In situations that appear more volatile, an immediate call to the police is in order, so the person can be hospitalized and receive attention from professionals trained in dealing with suicidal patients. Explore the legalities and admittance procedures at your local hospital before a crisis actually arises, so that you know what steps are required in order to keep a suicidal person safe during a vulnerable time. In some cases, the signature of a family member is needed to keep the at-risk person in the hospital.

An important, though potentially exhausting, part of pastoral care is coming alongside people in our congregation who have lost hope. Perhaps a spouse or a child has died, and the survivor wants to give up. These people desperately need the love and support of their church family. The pastoral call in these situations is to help restore people's hope. A good background resource on this kind of ministry is *Hope in Pastoral Care and Counseling* by Andrew D. Lester. The author brings out the importance of a theology of hope in pastoral care—how to embrace both hope and despair and how to deal with our anxiety about the future.

Equally important in all aspects of pastoral care is the setting of boundaries.

Setting Boundaries

Pastors are not called to absorb all of the pain experienced by their people. That would surely be destructive to ministry early on. Appropriately set and maintained boundaries are critical to ongoing ministry. One thing I find helpful when I sense I am acting like a sponge to others' pain is to tell myself that the pain is their pain, not mine; it is their situation that they need to work out, not mine; the problems are theirs that they leave my office with, not mine to bear. Now by this, I am not suggesting that pastors need to be callous toward people and their pain. Quite the contrary. Pastors need to empathize with the struggles of others, but assuming the problems of others will lead to self-destruction and does not offer any real help. Myrlene Hamilton states it well in *All I Need to Know about Ministry I Learned from Fly Fishing*:

> As Christian leaders we need to be compassionate toward those whom we serve, but we must learn to be dispassionate as well, so that we do not absorb the other person's pain. It's a boundary issue. We can do a lot for other people, but we can't take responsibility for them. They must take charge of their own feelings, decisions, and actions. They must respond to the Word of God for themselves. We can't do it for them. (p. 89)

Another important aspect of setting boundaries involves being able to identify personal connections with particular situations. It is helpful to ask, What within me is being hooked by this particular case? What am I wrestling with that looks like their situation? What plank do I need to take out of my eye before trying to work on the speck in their eye? And, where does my issue end and theirs begin?

This differentiation between ourselves and the one to whom we are ministering is essential to effective ministry. Without differentiation, we will subconsciously project our own problem on them and try to solve it in them. Obviously, this does not work; it only adds extra stress to the person coming to us for counsel. For more help in learning about the self in ministry, I recommend that pastors take one or more continuing education units in clinical pastoral education. For a branch of the Association for Clinical Pastoral Education in your area, check the Web at www.acpe.edu.

Setting healthy boundaries is difficult, but very important, so pastors need to work hard at it. The process also needs to be grounded in prayer, so it is wise to remember to come often to the throne of grace to draw on that power that is beyond our own and to make sure we are on the correct assignment.

> Are you tired? Worn Out? Burned out on religion? Come to me. Get away with me and you'll recover your life. I'll show you how to take a real rest. Walk with me and work with me—watch how I do it. Learn the unforced rhythms of grace. I won't lay anything heavy or ill-fitting on you. Keep company with me and you'll learn to live freely and lightly. (Matthew 11:28-29, THE MESSAGE)

Recommended Resources

Association for Clinical Pastoral Education. www.acpe.edu.

Cook, Jerry, with Stanley C. Baldwin. *Love, Acceptance and Forgiveness: Equipping the Church to be Truly Christian in a Non-Christian World*. Ventura, Calif.: Regal Books, 1979.

Estadt, Barry K. *Pastoral Counseling*. Englewood Cliffs, N.J.: Prentice-Hall, Inc., 1983.

Fortune, Marie M. *Sexual Abuse Prevention: A Study for Teenagers*. New York, N.Y.: United Church Press, 1986 edition.

Fortune is also the executive director of the Center for the Prevention of Sexual and Domestic Violence, which is in the process of changing its name to Faith Trust Institute. For current material listings go to www.cpsdv.org. This site also lists videos available, such as *Domestic Violence: What Churches Can Do*; *The Healing Years*; and *A Sacred Trust: Boundary Issues for Clergy and Spiritual Teachers*.

Hamilton, Myrlene L. J. *All I Need to Know about Ministry I Learned from Fly Fishing*. Valley Forge, Pa.: Judson Press, 2001.

Heggen, Carolyn Holderread. *Sexual Abuse in Christian Homes and Churches*. Scottsdale, Ariz.: Herald Press, 1993.

Howe, Leroy. *A Pastor in Every Pew: Equipping Laity for Pastoral Care*. Valley Forge, Pa.: Judson Press, 2000.

Leehan, James. *Pastoral Care for Survivors of Family Abuse*. Louisville, Ky.: Westminster/John Knox Press, 1989.

Lester, Andrew D. *Hope in Pastoral Care and Counseling*. Louisville, Ky.: Westminster/John Knox Press, 1995.

London, H. B., Jr. and Neil Wiseman. *They Call Me Pastor*. Ventura, Calif.: Regal Books, 2000. (Available from the Church Growth Institute at 800-553-GROW.)

Seymour, Jody. *A Time for Healing: Overcoming the Perils of Ministry*. Valley Forge, Pa.: Judson Press, 1995.

CHAPTER 5

Conflict Management

THE WORD *CONFLICT* MAY BE UNDERSTOOD IN MANY DIFFER-
ent ways. Conflict can be a struggle between individuals
or groups of people over a common prize. It may be dif-
fering viewpoints on how something can best be done. It may simply be resistance to change. In any case, conflict is primarily rela-
tional with the differences among the people involved ranging from
mild disagreement to full-scale war. Conflict is also a normal part
of living with other people and facing life's changes. Conflict is not
evil or sinful in itself. It is when conflict is managed poorly that it
can lead to sinful behavior, chaos, or even disaster. When managed
well, conflict can become a wonderful catalyst for positive change
and growth. Conflict in the church has this potential. Given human
nature and until we get to heaven, we will have a tendency to com-
pete with one another over a goal, over ways of doing things, or in
order to show who is in charge. Giving in to this aspect of human
nature can lead to destructive handling of conflict, as most readers
are probably aware.

It is especially important to manage conflict well in the church,
so that we do not destroy ourselves. One thing to learn about conflict is that there will be lots of opportunities for managing it in the
church. This is especially true as church people face change, which
is something most of us do not like, because, among other things,
it really stretches our faith. This resistance to change alone can produce conflict. Since we know that change is a constant in our
world, the question becomes, How are we going to manage it? In
the church it is helpful to approach change in such a way as to

minimize the potential for conflict. Five suggestions for managing change and its potential conflict are: lead change, empower natural leaders, watch out for well-intentioned dragons, avoid triangulation, and utilize church discipline.

Lead Change

Ignoring change and hoping it will go away without causing conflict is not an effective strategy. Change is inevitable, so it is better to take charge and manage change before it causes serious conflict. A crucial tool for managing change is preparation. It takes time to explain a new concept and implement any change in the church. People like advanced warning when something new is coming. I have found it very helpful to seed ideas before I need a final decision on a proposed change. For example, I bring up the needed change as an idea in principle first and ask the following questions: Are we interested in doing this? What are the advantages and disadvantages of this change and what are the advantages and disadvantages of not changing? What are alternatives and their pros and cons?

Bouncing ideas around without the pressure to make a final decision takes a tremendous amount of stress away from the issue. Likewise, having a follow-up meeting to get used to the idea of change goes a long way in making an idea more acceptable. This strategy also brings the leadership team up to speed through all the wrestling already done on an issue and lays the groundwork for making a sound decision together. In addition to laying this groundwork, it is essential that the pastor have enough background on any proposal to speak intelligently about it. Useful information can be interjected as needed while pastors listen to the opinions of the decision makers. Having done homework ahead of time will serve change well.

The church leadership will ultimately be key in bringing about needed change. One important strategy for introducing change and minimizing conflict is good timing. Begin by measuring the readiness of the congregation for any proposed change, making sure that all concerns have been sufficiently addressed. Bad planning can allow major blockages to the change to come up unexpectedly at the final vote. It may be necessary, depending on the church's readiness to accept a change, to wait for a better time to implement a change and thereby minimize conflict. A very helpful resource on assessing readiness level and choosing leadership style accordingly is Hersey and Blanchard's book, *Management of Organizational Behavior: Utilizing Human Resources.* Blanchard also has a delightful series on working with people entitled *The One-Minute Manager.* These books are about 100 pages in length and are presented in story form.

Part of the assessment process of congregational readiness is the pastor's awareness of his or her own potential influence in leading change. An analogy that I have found helpful is the concept of poker (now stay with me on this). Most of us are familiar with the logistics of poker (perhaps not too familiar, though). The idea is that each player begins with a number of poker chips. In each round of the game, players either earn or lose chips. How successfully players manage their chips determines how long they remain in the game. Through the process of coming to a new church, a new pastor receives a certain number of chips. This is generally a substantial amount since most churches look forward to having a new minister in place. Thus a honeymoon phase begins and even if the new pastor makes mistakes, losing a few chips does not endanger the large number on hand. In some ways, making changes at this phase is easiest, since the pastor has so many chips. The adage not to make changes during the first year may not always be the soundest advice. However, should the candidating weekend not go well or should the vote in favor be low (less then 80 percent), fewer chips are given to the new pastor and the honeymoon will not last as long. Making lots of changes right away in this case would be risky. More chips must be earned before changes are made.

As the pastor serves the church, chips are earned or lost. Offering support and encouragement to church people in their suffering and having parishioners accept that support earns chips. Preaching sound, relevant sermons earns chips. Doing the job well in any area earns chips. Conversely, not being there for someone who is hurting, bungling something important, not being well prepared for several sermons, not being available on a regular basis, and leading changes that produce bad results for the church all lose chips. The key, then, when it comes to leading change, is to have a good idea of the number of chips on hand. The more chips, the greater the risk that can be safely taken. The fewer the chips, the less change the pastor should personally spearhead. Another way of saying this is "Choose your battles wisely."

While assessing the number of chips on hand is somewhat subjective, there are two sources on which to draw. One is our inner sense, as quickened by the Holy Spirit and through prayerful questions such as: How is my rapport with the church and its current leadership? How well has my ministry been going lately? Will people follow me in another change right now? What is my gut level feeling about this new change? It is important for pastors to trust their God-given instincts. The other source of information is trusted individuals in the church who have a good sense of where the church-pastor relationship stands. The responses received in prayer and from trusted church members will provide a good idea of the number of chips a pastor has on hand.

This analogy provides a picture only to aid in assessing timing for implementing change. Other parts of the poker analogy are *not* helpful. These include trying to bluff and risking everything. For example, it is very poor practice for a pastor to carry around a resignation letter and use it to get his or her way. Eventually someone will call the bluff, accept the letter, and end that pastor's tenure. Pastors need to learn to wisely lead change and not use manipulation.

Since good communication is a key element in successfully implementing change and in resolving conflict, I recommend

Communication and Conflict Management in Churches and Christian Organizations by Kenneth Gangel and Samuel Canine. My personal favorite writer on church leadership and change is Lyle Schaller. A prolific writer, he has penned some fifty books on a variety of aspects of church life. I was introduced to Schaller through what is an old book now, *The Change Agent*, and have fully enjoyed him ever since. Somewhat newer books by him that I would recommend are *Strategies for Change* and *Activating the Passive Church: Diagnosis and Treatment*.

Empower Natural Leaders

Each congregation has its share of natural leaders. A natural leader is one whose wisdom the congregation tends to listen to, even if the person may normally be soft-spoken. Natural leaders may be persons with knowledge of the history of the church and of what things have been tried before. Or they may be people whom the congregation simply trusts. Conflict tends to emerge when these natural leaders place their weight against a proposed change. A wise pastor will quickly identify these potential blockers, then work to win them over and empower them to lead change. This is called *ownership*. If a pastor can show key leaders the value of a particular change for the whole church before the change is voted down, the chances of it passing and lasting greatly increase. Again, this is part of doing the homework designed to lessen the conflict that often accompanies implementing change. In her book *All I Need to Know about Ministry I Learned from Fly Fishing*, Myrlene Hamilton addresses the related issue of learning to "trust the locals." A helpful model for building ownership that is drawn from a business perspective can be found in Max DePree's book, *Leadership Is an Art*.

Watch Out for Well-intentioned Dragons

As much as some of us don't like to admit it, there are dragons in the church, although many have good intentions. Dragons are people who are *very* vocal and blow fire (iceman, cousin to the dragon, dumps cold water) on every new ministry idea with which they do not agree. While dragons often think they have the best interests of God and the church in mind, they often serve the same role as the religious leaders in Jesus' day, who kept Christ's teachings out of their synagogues and religious practices.

Well-intentioned dragons need to be handled carefully. Slaying them is not exercising Christian love. Putting them in their proper place, however, is godly tough love. I would suggest using a pattern of church discipline drawn from Matthew 18:15-17:

- Go to them in private and talk about how their stand is harming the church as a whole. Much difficulty arises from poor communication or feelings of having been overlooked during a decision process. Some dragons will change when given the opportunity to be heard.
- If they will not listen, take representatives from the deacon board who are selected based on their ability to be objective and try again. It now becomes a team confronting the dragon, rather than just the pastor.
- If there is still no change, take the matter to the governing body of the church.
- With the wisdom and backing of the governing body of the church, carefully and lovingly take the matter to the church membership.
- In all steps, seek *reconciliation* rather than victory over the dragon.

Admittedly, some dragons are not manageable. Many have destroyed churches or pastors in order to keep their power. In some of these cases, bringing in a conflict management team from outside the church can be effective and many denominations have such teams. In either case, it is vital to seek to challenge the unacceptable *behavior* rather than the person. Pastors should seek reconciliation rather than separation, but lead where necessary, bathing the entire process in personal and communal prayer. (See the Recommended Resources at the end of this chapter for some helpful books on dealing with difficult people.)

Avoid Triangulation

Triangulation is becoming caught between two quarreling parties. In these cases, each side meets with the pastor privately, presents an impassioned case, and seeks to draw the pastor in to support his or her side of the argument. Often, when a pastor tries to remain neutral, both parties turn on the pastor. The best approach is to avoid being drawn into triangulation. Just as siblings sometimes need to work differences out themselves, so do people in the church. Pastors can mediate when it is possible to bring both parties together, but we still need to resist taking sides in any disagreement. It is especially important to watch out for the subtleties of master manipulators who specialize in drawing people in unawares.

Most pastors have already experienced attempts to triangulate them. Examples include involving the pastor as a third party in a conversation, rather than addressing the individual with whom there is a difficulty; trying to manipulate or bias the facts of a situation to swing the pastor (as a third party) to favor one position over another; or trying to attain control over another individual by aligning with the pastor, who is perceived as a powerful person to have on one's side. Learn to sense these political maneuvers and to back away gracefully, realigning the conversation between the two who are having the difficulty so that they are compelled to talk it out themselves.

Utilize Church Discipline

I touched on the process of church discipline above, but more needs to be said. I want to state very strongly that the goal of utilizing church discipline is always reconciliation rather than meting out discipline. The process is not about punishment. Eternal consequences are God's job. Too often people dwell on what punishment is appropriate for a given "crime." A healthier perspective is to ask, What encouragement, counsel, admonition, or consequence is most likely to turn this person around and restore our fellowship with them?

Another difficult task of church discipline is deciding which cases warrant this action. Many churches today tend to avoid or delay confronting problems, but we are not alone in this hesitance. The church in Corinth way back in Paul's time struggled with the same procrastination (1 Corinthians 5:1-5), and Paul scolded them for it. Part of shepherding the flock involves discipline. Areas that warrant correction toward reconciliation are doctrinal impurity such as denying the divinity of Christ, sins of human character such as moral impurity, or any flagrant sin that is deliberately and publicly practiced without repentance. Each church usually has some indication in its constitution or bylaws as to when, or under what circumstances, church discipline is to be applied. Hopefully, a restoration process is outlined as well.

A helpful case study of an effective intervention and restoration is found in Don Baker's *Beyond Forgiveness: The Healing Touch of Church Discipline*. Baker presents the story of how one congregation ministered to a member of its staff who had fallen into sin, ultimately leading to healing and restoration.

In closing, let me reiterate that the discipline process begins privately with the individual in the hope that reconciliation will happen before it needs to come to the church as a whole.

Recommended Resources
Baker, Don. *Beyond Forgiveness: The Healing Touch of Church Discipline*. Portland, Ore. Multnomah Press, 1984.

Blanchard, Kenneth and Margret McBride. *The One-Minute Apology: A Powerful Way to Make Things Better*. New York, N.Y.: HarperCollins Publishers, Inc., 2003. (See also Blanchard's *The One-Minute Manager* series. These books are about 100 pages in length and are told profoundly in story form.)

Bramson, Robert M. *Coping with Difficult People*. Garden City, NJ: Anchor Press/Doubleday, 1981.

DePree, Max. *Leadership Is an Art*. New York, N.Y.: Dell Publishing, 1989.

Gangel, Kenneth O., and Samuel L. Canine. *Communication and Conflict Management in Churches and Christian Organizations*. Nashville, Tenn.: Broadman Press, 1992.

Hamilton, Myrlene L. J. *All I Need to Know about Ministry I Learned from Fly Fishing*. Valley Forge, Pa.: Judson Press, 2001.

Hersey, Paul and Kenneth H. Blanchard. *Management of Organizational Behavior: Utilizing Human Resources*. Eighth ed. Englewood Cliffs, N.J.: Prentice-Hall, 2000.

Meier, Paul, M.D. *Don't Let Jerks Get the Best of You: Advice for Dealing with Difficult People*. Nashville, Tenn.: Thomas Nelson Publishers, 1993.

Schaller, Lyle E. *The Change Agent*. Nashville, Tenn.: Abingdon Press, 1972.

———. *Activating the Passive Church: Diagnosis and Treatment*. Nashville, Tenn.: Abingdon Press, 1981.

————. *Strategies for Change.* Nashville, Tenn.: Abingdon Press, 1993.

Shelley, Marshall. *Well-Intentioned Dragons: Ministering to Problem People in the Church.* Minneapolis, Minn.: Bethany House Publishers, 1994.

CHAPTER 6

Team Ministry

"**M**Y JOB WOULD BE PERFECT IF I JUST DIDN'T HAVE TO work with people!" I think we all feel this way at times, but working with fallible people is a pastor's job. We are a body and each part needs to learn how to work with the other parts, as the apostle Paul wrote:

> [S]peaking the truth in love, we are to grow up in all aspects into Him, who is the head, even Christ, from whom the whole body, *being fitted and held together* by that which *every joint supplies*, according to the *proper working of each individual part*, causes the growth of the body for the building up of itself in love. (Ephesians 4:15-16, NAS, emphasis mine)

Part of the pastor's job is to encourage each part to work properly. This involves working with paid staff, with volunteers, and across generational lines. (The importance of staff meetings is addressed in chapter seven.)

Working with Paid Staff

The goal of having staff is to accomplish more work together than what any one person can do alone. A spirit of teamwork is essential to accomplish this goal. I prefer to have a paragraph in each staff job description, including my own, that spells out this philosophy. My current job descriptions for pastoral staff all include the following paragraph:

This position is to be reviewed annually by the Pastoral Relations Committee. It is hoped that in our growing church there would be a "team ministry" with the highest degree of cooperation between the ministerial staff, secretary, and all other leaders and workers in the total church programs. It is understood that the _____ Pastor will adhere to the Code of Ministerial Ethics formulated by the Ministers' Council of the ABC/USA.

It is always an interesting question as to when pastoral staff should be added in a church. A general rule of thumb has been to have one pastor per 100 members, with the second full-time staff member being added at the 150 to 250 membership level. Each church will need to work out this timing question for their own situation in light of their needs and financial abilities. Some churches opt to add part-time staff earlier, rather than waiting until they can afford a full-time person. Availability of quality leadership is a factor; for example, if a seminary is nearby, a part-time field placement for a pastoral student can work well. So too can hiring a retired pastor who lives in the area. Churches need to explore the resources available and work out the best plan for their situations.

Often the first pastoral staff person added is someone specialized in youth ministry. Some churches prefer an associate or assistant pastor so that he or she can handle more ministry responsibilities than simply youth work. Other churches prefer to hire a musician, such as a choir conductor, organist, or minister of worship. Whichever direction is chosen, a clear job description is essential. Good job descriptions include expectations, lines of accountability, and terms of performance evaluation, so that it is clear who is responsible to whom and for what. This is especially important in multi-staff settings. The job description also helps clarify each person's area of responsibility on the team so as to avoid unnecessary overlaps and to help all team members fulfill their position for the good of the church as a whole. Having all this information clear up-front also makes annual evaluation, daily interaction, and cooperation much easier.

It is also very helpful to get a good sense of a new staff member's philosophy of ministry during the interview process to see if it is compatible with the existing staff's philosophy. If, for example, one pastor is set on traditional worship and the other on contemporary music only, therein lies a potential problem. Likewise, if one pastor wishes to coddle the flock and the other desires to stir them up, a compromise needs to be worked out. Clarifying compatibility and negotiating goals and direction before hiring an individual can head off problems. A helpful book for working out details related to adding staff is *Let's Talk about Church Staff Relationships* by Ronald Wiebe and Bruce Rowlison.

Another area that warrants consideration is dual clergy couples. My wife and I are both ordained clergy and have experienced an interesting and varied dance as we have worked out our careers. Currently we work at the same church. This is a first for us. I serve as the lead pastor and she is the executive director of a parish-based Clinical Pastoral Education Center in our church. Throughout our marriage of 22 years, we have learned that flexibility and team-work, rather than competition, are key. Myrlene Hamilton also serves as part of a dual clergy couple and gives some helpful suggestions for working things out in her book, *All I Need to Know about Ministry I Learned from Fly Fishing*.

In addition to pastoral staff, pastors also often work with secretarial and custodial staff. Secretarial staff requires supervision by and close cooperation with the minister. A healthy relationship here, in every way, will make this staffing set-up most effective. When the pastor and secretary are of the opposite sex, there need to be clear, respected boundaries and reevaluation of the relationship if it becomes awkward. One way to do this is to agree that either party may call a "relationship check" should he or she feel uneasy about something. For example, simply saying "I think I need a relationship check because something is bothering me about how we are relating to each other" is a nonthreatening way to begin and one that shows personal ownership of the concern. Flagging it this way means the two talk about any "weirdness" they feel, so to maintain integrity in the relationship. This tactic is also important for working with any full-time ministerial staff. It takes intentional work and complete honesty to keep healthy boundaries.

If a custodian is on staff, it is helpful to have someone else, such as a trustee, oversee that work and be responsible for needed supplies. This arrangement should be clear in the job description. While the pastor can be a support for custodial staff as individuals, pastors should avoid following them around and talking the entire time they are trying to do their job.

Working with Volunteers

Working with volunteers presents a variety of challenges to pastors, because volunteers are unpaid, may have expertise the pastor does not have, and in some cases, may be highly opinionated. Since paid pastors often work with a variety of unpaid volunteers, from Sunday school teachers to managing boards to worship leaders and building-maintenance help, the pastoral leadership style that works best is that of gentle influence rather than that of demands. Since leading by influence can take much longer to get things done, it can be very frustrating; however, issuing orders without allowing time for volunteers to build personal ownership of a given project is a quick track to failure.

Good communication is essential in working with volunteers. It is important that they clearly understand what is expected of them. It is common to assume that volunteers understand what is required only to find them doing a job completely differently than expected. Sometimes this works out, if pastors and/or the outcomes are flexible. Other times, jobs need to be redone, which risks volunteers getting hurt feelings. It is important to try to avoid hurting feelings by being clear in the beginning and by matching volunteers carefully to tasks for which they are qualified. It is wise when planning to keep in mind that it is quite difficult to "fire" a volunteer.

Given the diversity of people in the typical congregation, another challenge of working with volunteers is that some may have more expertise than the pastor in a particular area. This can be especially true when it comes to running the sound system or keeping up with ever-changing technology. Pastors need to decide if they will trust lay people with technical things that might affect their presentations, such as a Power Point presentation of a sermon, keeping in mind that the most skilled volunteer may still be in high school. Allowing volunteers across ages to use their giftedness to glorify God is a precious gift to them and to the church. Pastors just need to tighten down those personal shock absorbers and trust.

A particularly difficult challenge is working with opinionated volunteers. These people may not have superior skills, but nonetheless they feel very strongly about how things are to be done. For example, involving lay volunteers in music as well as in Scripture readings and prayers can greatly enhance worship services, but music and worship can often test a pastor's commitment to working with volunteers. Most people tend to have very strong preferences about worship music. When working with a wide range of views among the volunteers or if a worship leader differs significantly in style from the pastor, much care must be taken to build teamwork. Negotiation is a vital tool for this. It means spending extra time to explain and build a corporate philosophy of worship, so that giftedness and need are best matched.

Pastors need to learn to work with volunteers in every area of church life. Although pushing and prodding are sometimes needed, it is also wise to lead by example. The old adage "Don't ask a volunteer to do something you wouldn't be willing to do yourself"

is helpful to keep in mind. Just because pastors are "trained clergy," it doesn't mean we should always keep our hands from getting dirty. No work should be beneath a pastor. Christ, who was
even willing to wash the dirty feet of his volunteers, is our example. As Jesus said, that example is for us and if we know these
things, we are blessed if we do them (see John 13:14-17).

It is amazing what bonds of loyalty can develop with volunteers
when we roll up our sleeves and get right in there with them. Does
this mean that pastors should always do all the most menial jobs?
No, it does not. There still is room for delegation, so that pastors
can dedicate time and energy to the demands of the job. It is important, then, to allow the person who is assigned the job to vacuum
the sanctuary to do so, and the pastor should always be cordial,
encouraging, and willing to offer a word of thanks. Gratitude and
support go a long way in helping volunteers feel good about their
service, and this affirmation encourages a job well done. (For additional insights in working with volunteers, see the Recommended
Resources at the end of this chapter.)

Working Across Generation Lines

The story is told of a pastor who was having a dream in which he
was talking to God about the people in his congregation. God
commented that the pastor seemed to know only about sixty-per-
cent of the congregation by name. Somewhat flustered because it
was a small church, the pastor questioned what God meant. To
which God replied, "Name three people in your church under
three." The pastor could not do it and he had to admit he really
had not paid attention to the children of his congregation.

God has entrusted pastors with the care of all ages in the church.
A wise pastor asks, Am I seeing to it that each age groups' needs
are met by me or by someone else? Pastoral contact across age levels is important. One challenge I take on each week is to tell the
children's story in church. It is wonderful what the children come

up with in response to my questions. During that brief interaction, the children learn that I am safe and approachable. How critical that is for their future involvement in the church. I also make a special point of talking to the seniors on Sundays before the service, since they are often early, or as they come through the greeting line afterwards. It is a simple matter to show care and concern and requires just a little effort. Pastors need to intentionally work at relating with all the people in the church, even when others have the primary task of working with specific age groups.

Recommended Resources

George, Carl F. and Robert E. Logan. *Leading and Managing Your Church*. Old Tappan, N.J.: Fleming H. Revell Company, 1987. (Revell is now a division of Baker Books)

Hamilton, Myrlene L. J. *All I Need to Know about Ministry I Learned from Fly Fishing*. Valley Forge, Pa.: Judson Press, 2001 (especially pp. 39–40).

Johnson, Douglas W. *The Care and Feeding of Volunteers,* in Lyle Schaller's "Creative Leadership" series. Nashville, Tenn.: Abingdon Press, 1978.

McDonough, Reginald M. *Working with Volunteer Leaders in the Church*. Nashville, Tenn.: Broadman Press, 1976.

"The One-Minute Manager" series. Blanchard, Kenneth, and various coauthors. New York, N.Y.: HarperCollins Publishers, Inc., various dates.

Wiebe, Ronald W., and Bruce A. Rowlison. *Let's Talk about Church Staff Relationships*. Lebanon, Tenn.: Green Leaf Press, 1983.

Your Church: Helping You with the Business of Ministry. Mike Schreiter, managing editor. (A free publication to church addresses from Christianity Today International. Write to *YOUR CHURCH*, P.O. Box 2023, Langhorne, PA 19047, or try online at www.yourchurch.net.)

CHAPTER 7

Administration

M INISTRY HAS MANY DEMANDS, AND ONE OF THE MOST relentless is that of administration. The church is very similar to a business in this respect. Bills need to be processed and paid, phone calls need to be made, correspondence needs to be written, and connections need to be created between various agencies within the church. In addition, a flow of information needs to be created so that good communication takes place within the congregation. In this chapter we will look at the practical issues of accountability and time management, processing written materials, creating a positive office spirit, and managing special projects.

Accountability and Time Management

With all of the demands placed on pastors, some form of reporting and accountability is essential for effective time management. Record keeping can be mundane, however, and not necessarily clear-cut. It can be difficult sometimes to sort out what constitutes "work" and what does not. For example, should talking to a parishioner for a half hour at the grocery store on the pastor's day off be recorded as work time? Even with these limitations, making the effort to keep track of where the hours go can be helpful, so let's begin with a look at three manageable approaches to logging pastoral work. Appendix D provides sample logs for the following first and second approaches.

One way to track work time is to keep a time log for one week out of each month, recording time spent within general ministry categories. Keeping a log one week per month provides an idea of how many hours are spent working, how they are spent, and how time use compares with ministry expectations. Even this amount of data can be useful for discussing job performance with a Pastoral Relations Committee or accountability board. Recording this information every week would be even more helpful, but that could be overwhelmingly tedious. Who wants to categorize and record how every minute is spent? Recording one week per month should be doable without being overwhelming.

An old saying goes, "It's not so much the hours you put in, but what you put into the hours, that counts." The idea here is to pay attention to quality, rather than mere quantity. While the tracking form mentioned above primarily measures quantity, a way to measure quality is to maintain a list of activities in a given month. This type of reporting focuses on completed activities rather than on hours put in. I am currently experimenting with recording the number of sermons preached, classes taught, special services led, meetings attended, hospital visits, and so on. While tracking some of the smaller details, such as phone calls, can be tedious, keeping cumulative numbers can provide some valuable data. For example, keeping track of the number of visitor letters sent out shows how many people actually visited the church each month and for the year.

A third way to be accountable for time use is to simply meet monthly with a small group to discuss how the week or month has gone. This meeting can be informal, and reporting can be verbal with all involved being free to offer praise or to raise concerns. The Pastoral Relations Committee (or comparable accountability board) can service this purpose. As with all committees, an accountability committee is only as good as the people on the committee. Such a committee requires trustworthy participants in whom the pastor can confide.

While accountability is one tool that can help pastors manage time, so too can good planning. I find it very helpful to generate a schedule at the beginning of the week of all the things that need to be done that week. Since many responsibilities repeat weekly, I use my computer for this and find it easy to simply update the same form each week. Helpful categories for this task include things to do (pastor's responsibility), things to organize (tasks that can be delegated), things to check on (tasks that have been delegated), meetings to attend, phone calls to make, and people to visit. I also organize each day according to the priority of each task for that day, starting with the most important. This way priority items are accomplished, even if everything on the list is not. I find that checking off completed tasks motivates me and provides me with a feeling of accomplishment as the day progresses.

Here's one final thought on planning. Any list of things to do includes items that we especially dislike. I suggest tackling those first to get them out of the way and to remove the burden of them. That way the rest of the day can be enjoyed. If undesirable or difficult tasks are left to the end of the day, the subconscious mind may work overtime to keep us from getting that far on the list. It can be amazing how much time the other tasks will consume, dragging on until no time is left for the undesirable, yet necessary tasks—similar to how all kinds of things "need" to be done before beginning work on income tax returns. When the unpleasant tasks are tackled first, the remaining items go more efficiently. There are many time management books on the market today. I have several on my bookshelf that I have not yet read (didn't have the time), but I have included two that look promising in this chapter's resource list.

Processing Written Materials

Even small churches receive many pieces of mail daily. In a church that receives ten pieces of mail a day and does not have a secretary, a pastor who takes Monday off will arrive on Tuesday to find twenty pieces of mail waiting to be sorted. This can give the feeling of being behind just as the week is beginning. Sorting mail over the garbage can to eliminate junk mail can expedite the process. Other items can be sorted into categories such as materials that need further review (magazines and journals), items to be filed for future reference (sermon ideas), bills that need to be passed on immediately to the treasurer, resources for other church leaders (youth materials), tithe checks from vacationing members (always a joy) that need to be safely stored, and regular mailings from denominational offices, often with forms to be filled out and returned or involving information that needs to be communicated to the congregation. Without secretarial help, this is a formidable task, and even with administrative help, ultimately much still needs to be processed by the pastor.

By the way, you know all that "good stuff" that is pulled from the debris of junk mail? I have come up with a system that makes it possible to actually find those items when I need them. I have a "Special Day" section in a file drawer in which I keep separate folders for not only the typical categories of Christmas and Easter, but also for little tidbits related to Maundy Thursday, Good Friday, Thanksgiving, Labor Day, Christian Unity Sunday, Mother's Day, Father's Day, and special seasons of the church year. I also find it helpful to keep individual files for jokes, quotes, poems, and illustrations. Numbering each item as it comes in and keeping a table of contents at the front of each file makes it possible for me to retrieve what I need when I need it. I also date each item when I use it.

In addition to processing all the materials that come to a church, pastors are faced with a variety of items that need to be processed out. These include correspondence, newsletters, church bulletins, and denominational forms. The goal is to create a healthy flow of accurate information throughout and beyond the church. Whether written communication is going outside the church or staying within the congregation, effort should be made to make it clear, concise, and neat. Just as attention is paid to formal business letters in order to represent the church well, so too should internal communications be accurate and attractive. Any task that is worthy of our time is worth doing well, so sloppiness is not appropriate at any point, even though internal communications are often reinforced verbally.

Individual styles vary, so pastors need to experiment and find a paper processing system that works for them. One way to handle incoming and outgoing mail is to set aside one hour (or whatever amount is required) each working day to deal with mail. If this time coincides with when the mail arrives, so much the better. Consistency makes the task less burdensome, enables the important things to be dealt with quickly, and insures that each piece of mail is sorted only once. Another approach is to set aside one or two half days per week to deal with administration. This method can be effective, but it is more challenging, since the "horizontal filing system" (spread out on any available flat surface) will be substantial by then. An established time works especially well for developing the weekly bulletin or the monthly newsletter, so that contributors can know when to submit their materials for inclusion.

In some churches, business administrators (paid or volunteer) handle the daily operating details of the church. With effective partnering, a good executive secretary can also be very valuable for administration. Hand writing responses to incoming mail directly on the original letters and having someone else compose and type up the response can save a lot of time. If processing written material is simply not a particular pastor's cup of tea, it is probably necessary just to make time to do it and get it out of the way first thing in the morning.

Creating a Positive Office Spirit

The atmosphere generated from the church during the week, whether over the phone or in the reception area, speaks volumes about that church. It can be a positive or negative witness, so creating a positive office spirit goes a long way in advertising a warm and friendly church. Consider, for instance, basic telephone courtesy. Telemarketing calls come to the church at what often seems the most inopportune time, and while it may be tempting to be obnoxious to the caller, that response is not appropriate to the office of pastor. So, especially for pastors who do not have secretaries to screen calls, it is important to remain polite while being firm. This same office demeanor is appropriate for church secretaries and pastors. Any church representative who is rude (slamming down the phone, etc.) does not reflect well on Christ. If state or national "Do Not Call" lists are available in your area, they can help filter out unwanted calls. Another option is to have a policy stating that the church does not respond to telephone solicitations.

The response to any call reflects on the church, giving the caller his or her first impression of what the church is about. First impressions are not retractable. It is especially important for responses to calls requesting pastoral care to be kind, gentle, and pastoral, with the receiver practicing good listening skills. Pastors may even need to learn to pray over the phone with those who need that special touch. There are also times when it is necessary to be firm and set boundaries when a call has gone on long enough and other ministry needs require attention.

Similar rules of courtesy apply to people who drop by the church. All persons, whether a stranger making a delivery, a needy person seeking help, or a parishioner needing pastoral care, should be received in a manner that reflects God's love and the church's warmth. These interactions present challenging opportunities to glorify God in word and deed.

A positive office spirit goes beyond courtesy and general atmosphere; it also depends on cultivation of smooth efficiency for office staff. "Dumping" large assignments on team members at 4:00 P.M. Fridays—assignments that *must* be out before the weekend, of course—does not build office spirit or aid efficiency. Consideration among staff members is essential.

One way to facilitate such consideration is for church staff to meet regularly—preferably at the same time, every week. Include the church secretary, custodian, and others, at least for the part of the meeting when decisions relevant to their job will be made. In this way, staff can communicate about scheduling events on the church calendar, sharing event details up to a month in advance, planning projects, and making arrangements for mailings or room setup. This process helps avoid last-minute "surprises" for everyone. Carol Shearn, in her book *The Church Office Handbook,* also suggests that a pastor should spend at least ten minutes each morning with key staff, reviewing the day's schedules (p. 11).

Communication in the office is critical, and this includes learning one another's personal preferences. "Everyone is different. One pastor wants all his mail opened, with the junk mail thrown away, and he wants the phone dialed for him. Another pastor does not want any mail opened, [she] likes [her] correspondence typed in block style, and [she] is irritated by telephone messages from salespersons" (Shearn, p. 11). Learning one another's preferences and accommodating those preferences whenever possible goes a long way in helping an office run smoothly. Note, there is just as much value in the pastor learning staff preferences as there is in staff learning pastoral preferences. If we accommodate those preferences (written vs. verbal instructions, maximum advance notice, etc.) in the usual routine, staff are more likely to accommodate *us* when a real crisis situation arises and such preferences cannot be granted.

Gathering occasionally as a staff for fun also fosters positive office spirit. A wonderful example of this that I have experienced is a full-fledged coffee break on Friday mornings, when lay people brought in snacks for the entire staff. The break was a great morale booster, a time for everyone to connect, and an opportunity to feel appreciated.

Managing Special Projects

Three important points need to be made about the pastor and special projects, which can take the form of major building projects, fund raising drives, or new programming. These are: pastors should beware of becoming consumed by any given project, pastors need to involve others meaningfully in special projects, and pastors should choose carefully when and where they take a stand.

It is easy for pastors to become consumed by new projects. Special projects can be exciting and exhilarating. When aspects of the pastor's main calling, such as preparing quality sermons, fall by the wayside while the pastor spends time on a new project, it is an indication that priorities are off. Indeed special projects sometimes require extra hours, but the regular work must also continue. When a pattern develops of skimping on regular work to spend time with a favored project, changes are in order. God calls pastors to minister, not to carry out one single project.

Closely related to the danger of being consumed by a special project is the danger of allowing a church project to become the *pastor's* project. In any new project, it is imperative to involve others as early as possible, including during the planning stages. Doing so builds wider ownership of the project, which is critical for any project to succeed. Comments like "It's the pastor's pet project" are warning flags and suggest the need to broaden support and involvement in a project.

New projects always involve some type of change, and as mentioned earlier, change causes tension. God's leading is critical for selecting projects. If a pastor is certain that a given project is in God's will and the timing is right, then the project should be stood by and seen through with as much of the core leadership of the church as possible on board. Few projects, however, are worth losing a pastorate. Projects need to be carefully chosen based on their potential benefit to God's kingdom and the church, the resources available, the degree of change already experienced recently, and the level of support from leadership and the congregation. It is seldom wise for the pastor to take a stand on a project all alone. There are times to be prophetic and call the people forward, but pastors need to be sure the call is from God and not arising from their own personal agendas. Sadly, it is not unheard of for a pastor to become consumed by a building project, divert a great deal of his or her time to it because it is hard to get others to work at it, and then, having lost the role of pastor, end up leaving the church after the project is completed. Pastors need to take care not to let this happen.

Recommended Resources

Johnson, Emmett V. *The Work of the Pastoral Relations Committee*. Valley Forge, Pa.: Judson Press, 1983.

Jones, Kirk Byron. *Addicted to Hurry: Spiritual Strategies for Slowing Down*. Valley Forge, Pa.: Judson Press, 2003.

———. *Rest in the Storm: Self-Care Strategies for Clergy and Other Caregivers*. Valley Forge, Pa.: Judson Press, 2001.

Ministerial Leadership Commission, eds. *The Pastoral Relations Committee and the Church/Staff Relations Committee*. Valley Forge, Pa.: Ministerial Leadership Commission, American Baptist Churches USA, 1996. The New Pastoral Relations Committee Workbook came out in 2004.

Shearn, Carol R. *The Church Office Handbook: A Basic Guide to Keeping Order*. Wilton, Conn.: Morehouse-Barlow, 1986.

CHAPTER 8

Outside Affiliations

WHILE THERE IS ENOUGH ACTIVITY IN MOST CHURCHES TO keep pastors amply busy, involvement outside the confines of the church is important, not only as an extension of one's ministry, but also to help keep the larger picture in view. In this chapter, we will consider four types of involvement outside the local church. These are personal support groups, denominational responsibilities, ecumenical commitments, and community involvement.

Personal Support Groups

In chapter two, we looked at self-care and its importance for the person of the pastor. A significant aspect of self-care is having the regular support of friends. Opinions are divided as to whether pastors should have close friends inside or outside of the church they serve. Those who say that friends can come from inside the church point out that these are the people with whom the most time is spent and time is an important factor for building close relationships. They also observe that it can be difficult to find sufficient time to invest in relationships outside the church. Those in the opposite camp argue that it is risky to express personal feelings to people inside the church, because church members are well connected with one another and because personal sharing runs the risk of breaking confidentiality. For example, should a pastor be at odds with someone's friend or relative, it is possible that information will get back to the wrong person.

Those who oppose friendships in the church also argue that it is not healthy to discuss personal concerns with a parishioner, because at that point the pastor ceases to be pastor to that parishioner. There are other concerns related to having church friendships. These include maintaining relationships after leaving a church and whether or not it is ethical to continue contact after a new pastor arrives and the importance of not appearing to have favorites in the church. While pastors will differ on where they stand on the issue of friendship in the church, each pastor needs to find a personal balance that is healthy and effective.

Whatever the perspective, some pastors never get around to finding a support group or even a single trusted friend. Perhaps this is one of the reasons why the burnout rate among pastors is so high. I recommend that pastors find at least one close confidant (other than a spouse) with whom they can share freely and confidentially. I have found it very helpful to build this type of relationship with a pastor of another church. When pastors are "kindred spirits," they can offer significant support to one another. Being kindred spirits requires valuing each other's ministry, desiring each other's success, and not being competitive with one another. Readers should revisit chapter two for resources on developing a network of support in ministry.

Denominational Responsibilities

Not long after beginning a new position, a pastor can usually expect a call from a nominating committee asking him or her to serve on a denominational board or committee. New leaders are always needed, and new pastors are often seen as good candidates to fill positions. My suggestion is for pastors to take as much time as possible to settle into any new position before accepting a place on a denominational committee, and then to accept only positions that are in accordance with personal giftedness and interests. This is a matter of setting boundaries, and both of these boundaries are significant. Any person needs time to settle into a new position, learn the job, and come to love the people. A good beginning is very important, so pastors need to have permission to give this priority as long as needed, remembering after all, that serving the new church is the main calling.

In Deuteronomy 24:5, the Bible mandates that a man should not go to war for one year after being married. This seems like an applicable time line for taking on denominational responsibilities. Accepting an outside commitment just because someone is needed is not a good decision. Rather, pastors should wait for positions that are attractive to their interests and where they can really make a contribution out of their giftedness. Then accepting a position becomes a win-win situation for the pastor, the church, and the denomination.

Finally, any commitment outside the church needs approval from the church, even when it is within the denomination. This helps keep the church aware of denominational workings and puts the support of church members behind the time and effort the pastor will need to invest in the new responsibility. It also helps strengthen the link between the local church and the denomination, which carries additional benefits.

Ecumenical Commitments

Each pastor will need to decide for him or herself what priority to give to the local ministerium. This question will need to be addressed anew in each new placement. In some settings the ministerium is small and can become a lifeline of support for each pastor involved. It can lead to combined church events that demonstrate to the wider community that God's people can work together. In one of my pastorates, we had combined Sunday evening services once a quarter across five denominations that included Protestants and Roman Catholics. We enjoyed awesome worship experiences and gained insight into what God was doing in the larger picture.

In other settings, the ministerium may be so large that pastors feel insignificant. In some cases, this problem can be addressed by joining a ministerial subgroup, such as an evangelical or a regional ministerium group. There are even sermon preparation groups made up of pastors who use the same lectionary and link to each other on the internet. They share sermon ideas and illustrations and thereby enrich one another's sermons. This is a great resource for those weeks when extra duties, such as funerals, cut into sermon preparation time.

The value of any ministerium relationship will be affected, in part, by what the pastor puts into it and what priority it is given. Joint ecumenical projects, which range from major events like evangelistic crusades to small local events, such as community prayer walks, are also often available. Usually there are more opportunities than one pastor can take advantage of, so choices need to be made. A pastor's personal view of ecumenical involvement and available time will play a large role in determining these choices. The key is to choose wisely, rather than giving a blanket no or yes to everything.

Community Involvement

I once heard it said that a pastor was as well known in the community as a little league softball coach as he was as the pastor of the church. Was that good or bad? I suppose it depends on his reputation as a coach and how that affected his role as a pastor. One of the unique challenges of ministry is that it is easy to become surrounded by Christians. Pastors work at the church, meet with other believers in planning meetings, and can allow church life to take over all of life. It is important, therefore, to intentionally build relationships with people outside the church. Outside relationships allow the opportunity to share the faith and model outreach to members of the congregation.

Being involved in the community is worthy and beneficial for pastors and also for those who live nearby. Neighbors need to see that faith is part of daily life, not just for life in and at the church. Pastors need to be good citizens and make contributions to the communities in which they live. Part of the pastor's and church member's calling is to touch those around them, and it is important for pastors to model what it means to be a good neighbor.

Community involvement can take many forms. For some pastors it may be coaching, if they are good at it. Communities need coaches who value young people as individuals, teach true sportsmanship, and refuse to become consumed by performance. For others, involvement in the local school is a better fit and can take the form of participating in the parent-teacher association, being a scorekeeper at sporting events, or serving as a member on the school board. A recent study reported by *Christianity Today* revealed that of 1,956 African American congregations surveyed, almost 10 percent had a pastor who had held elected office (February 2004, p. 35). Some pastors write for local newspapers, while others head up special community projects. All are situations that need solid Christian influence. Again, pastors need to find situations that fit personal giftedness and interests and that do not result in the compromising, in time or conviction, of the primary calling to serve the church.

Recommended Resource
Smietana, Bob. "MegaShepherd" in *Christianity Today*, February 2004, p. 29–35. This relates the story of James Meeks.

CHAPTER 9

Transitions

TRANSITIONS ARE A NORMAL PART OF MINISTRY. FOR SOME pastors, transition means changing personal style and patterns of ministry to adapt to changes in the church. Flexibility is critical to long-term ministry in the same church. More often, transition involves moving to a different church. Whatever the case, transition produces feelings of vulnerability and fragility. In this chapter, we will explore the delicate process of leaving a church and the process of securing and beginning a new pastorate.

Leaving a Church

Just as a pastor responds to God's call in coming to a particular church, so too do pastors need to listen for God's call to move on. The question of when it is time to leave a current ministry is one that does not have a single answer. The process of assessing the time to leave is dynamic and dependent on a pastor's relationship with God. Pastors need to ask themselves if they are in tune with God's voice or if something is in the way. Often a call from God is not easy to hear. The human tendency is to want to leave sooner or stay longer. Seeking to know the right time can become a personal wrestling match with God. A willingness to leave or stay is critical to hearing what God wants. The decision of whether to stay or go deserves earnest petitioning of God every bit as much as did the decision to enter ministry at the current place of service.

Sometimes the people in the church take the choice out of a pastor's hands and, unfortunately, they do not always handle it in a pleasant manner. In churches that operate under a call rather than placement system, pastors can be fired. Even though the church people or leadership may strongly believe they are doing right for the church, firing the pastor is not always according to God's will and seldom is it carried out in Christian love. Termination can even be about something much bigger than the pastor with the pastor simply becoming caught in the wave of change or being made into a scapegoat. An important principle of ministry, then, is for pastors to do their best before God, and having done so, not to take it personally if the church people reject them.

I remember being caught in a political maneuver at my first church where, because the senior minister resigned, the leadership expected the whole staff to resign, even though that was not what the people of the church wanted. It was considered protocol, and I still think it was a lousy policy. Such a policy insures that there is no help for the church during their transition time. Pastors need to go with the call of the church's leadership, even in situations such as the one I experienced, and trust that God will be faithful to lead one to the next place of service.

When a pastor experiences a firing, personal counseling to work through feelings of anger and rejection is helpful and timely, since the support system of the church is no longer available. While it is initially helpful to discuss reasons for the dismissal in order to understand what happened, it is not wise to continue to process the firing with friends in the church. This is better done with a counselor and/or a pastoral denominational administrator. Several denominations have connections with ministry counseling centers that specialize in helping pastors work through transitions, heal, and prepare for new ministries.

Leaving a church is one of the more difficult tasks of pastoral ministry, especially if the work in a given position feels incomplete. Nonetheless it is wise to leave graciously and trust the remaining work to God. King David provided a good example when, because it was God's will, he willingly gave up his kingdom to Absalom, rather than split the kingdom (2 Samuel 15–18). God later returned the kingdom to David. Pastors need to allow God the same freedom in their lives, even if God chooses not to give the church back.

A pastor's greatest calling is to be faithful to God. The human tendency is to seek popularity and acceptance, but as Paul warned Timothy, we need to watch out for people who only want their ears tickled (2 Timothy 4:3-4). Though more difficult, the calling is to comfort the afflicted and afflict the comfortable, doing both in a genuine spirit of love. This means asking God regularly for a great love for God's people in God's church. This love will form a solid basis for effective ministry. By God's grace, pastors need to be vessels of God's love and seek the goal of effectiveness rather than merely efficiency. A pastor who is facing departure, by that same grace, needs to love the people to the very end of the pastoral tenure. This will result in finishing his or her race well.

Securing and Beginning a New Pastorate

Many denominations have procedures in place to facilitate connections between pastors and churches. The process often involves churches developing a profile of the pastor they need and pastors developing a profile of their gifts and strengths. The goal is to affect a good match between church and pastor.

For pastors, the great challenge of the process is that it requires waiting and trusting the process (or better, trusting God in the process), after preparing the profile. It usually is not acceptable for pastors to pursue placements directly with churches, although this seems to be changing in some venues. In fact, it is often word of mouth (someone who knows that a pastor is seeking being aware of a church that needs a pastor, and putting the two together) that moves the search process along more quickly. Networking can be done ethically. Sensitivity to the leading of the Holy Spirit in relationships and faithfulness is essential during the waiting process.

Complete honesty provides the best foundation for future ministry once correspondence has begun with a particular church. While there is a tendency for both church and pastor to put forth only the best picture, appropriately sharing weaknesses is critical to successful and long-term ministry together. Appropriate honesty involves asking pertinent questions that are stirred within by the Holy Spirit. This can be especially hard for those seeking a first pastorate, who may fear "messing up." Honesty is essential, in spite of fears. It will greatly minimize regrets later. Many pastors have found themselves reflecting, "If only I had asked about . . . ," after moving into a new position. As experience in ministry comes, openness and complete honesty often flow more naturally.

While being in dialogue with more than one church at a time is acceptable, candidating at more than one church goes against the ministerial ethics of a number of denominations. Such practice undermines the integrity of the process. Honesty requires working with a single church once the process has moved to the point of candidacy. Otherwise, the pastor is really just checking out a variety of situations and misleading the churches. This principle is equally true for churches. While the search committee will process candidates simultaneously, only one pastor should be presented to the church for candidacy at a time.

The groundwork for beginning a position well is laid during the search process. It is important that the pastor and church understand one another as fully as possible. Pastors need to make careful observations and thoroughly research the culture of the church during the exploration stage. This means (again) that it is wise to ask many questions, to reflect on the implications of the responses for future ministry, and to be careful not to take anything for granted.

Prospective pastors should consider the socioeconomic situation of a church in light of that to which they are accustomed. For example, if a pastor is moving to a blue-collar church and this represents a cultural shift, it is important to consider what adjustments need to be made. In *Blue-Collar Ministry*, Tex Sample seeks to help readers move beyond stereotypes, so that real ministry can happen. He lists fifteen basics for serving a blue-collar church, such as understanding that religion is important to blue-collar people as a way of meeting needs that are unanswered in secular society (p. 121). Understanding cultural phenomena can go a long way in helping pastors understand why people do what they do in the church and thereby provide significant help in preparing for new ministries.

Understanding individual church culture also involves studying a church's theology and practice. Knowing whether a congregation's theology is generally fundamental, conservative, liberal, or radical will not only impact the decision about accepting a position, it will also impact the goals a new pastor sets for ministry within a given congregation. An awareness of the theological leanings of the congregation can guide sermon preparation and help new pastors avoid unintentionally stirring up conflict.

Preparing for and beginning a new ministry also necessitates coming to understand what the church values. While traditions can become empty rituals, they can also be very meaningful and necessary experiences. In my own experience, for example, I have found that bagpipes at a funeral, which are not a personal favorite, can be extremely meaningful and comforting to others. Working with the church on issues of tradition and style of worship is essential. Slowly adapting a church's traditional service is better than disorienting people by changing it immediately and completely.

The key to a good beginning for effective pastoral ministry is for pastors to know and love the people as they are and within their cultural context, and then for pastor and church to move together toward becoming more the people of God as outlined in the Bible. See the Recommended Resources for other materials to help move through the stages of transition effectively—and graciously.

Recommended Resources

BOOKS

Marshall, Myra with Dan McGee and Jennifer Bryon Owen. *Beyond Termination*. Nashville, TN: Broadman Press, 1990.

Oswald, Roy M., James M. Heath, and Ann W. Heath. *Beginning Ministry Together: The Alban Handbook for Clergy Transitions*. Bethesda, Md.: Alban Institute, 2003. This is a practical handbook to help pastors work through all the stages of transition.

Sample, Tex. *Blue-Collar Ministry: Facing Economic and Social Realities of Working People*. Valley Forge, Pa.: Judson Press, 1984.

Woods, C. Jeff. *Better Than Success: 8 Principles of Faithful Leadership*. Valley Forge, Pa.: Judson Press, 2001.

WEBSITES

www.midwestministry.org. This site lists four locations of counseling centers specializing in helping clergy through transition.

www.ministerscouncil.com. A good site for networking in the ABC/USA. It also offers a variety of helps and resources, including a section on transitions and a discussion by Dr. Riley Walker on when it is time to move on from a church.

A Noble Task

The saying is sure: whoever aspires to the office of bishop [pastor/elder] desires a noble task. (1 Timothy 3:1)

Pastoral ministry is indeed a noble undertaking for those who are called of God. Those who would pursue pastoral ministry must make sure of their calling. Those who are uncertain of the call would be wise to try other vocations until they are drawn to the pastorate with the fervor that Jeremiah expressed.

And I can't stop! If I say I'll never mention the Lord or speak in his name, his word burns in my heart like a fire. It's like a fire in my bones! I am weary of holding it in! (Jeremiah 20:9, NLT)

Those who are certain of God's call to pastoral ministry must pursue it, first seeking the best training available, and then serve faithfully, bearing in mind the admonition of the apostle Peter:

And now a word to you who are elders in the churches. I, too, am an elder and a witness to the sufferings of Christ. And I, too, will share his glory and his honor when he returns. As a fellow elder, this is my appeal to you: Care for the flock of God entrusted to you. Watch over it willingly, not grudgingly—not for what you will get out of it, but because you are eager to serve God. Don't lord it over the people assigned to your care, but lead them by your good example. And when the head Shepherd comes, your reward will be a never-ending share in his glory and honor. (1 Peter 5:1-4, NLT)

May each of you who have accepted this noble task continually grow and carry out the work of the pastor according to how God has called and gifted you.

ABCUSA Ministerial Code of Ethics

THE COVENANT AND CODE OF ETHICS
for Ministerial Leaders of American Baptist Churches

Having accepted God's call to leadership in Christ's Church, I covenant with God to serve Christ and the Church with God's help, to deepen my obedience to the Two Great Commandments: to love the Lord our God with all my heart, soul, mind, and strength, and to love my neighbor as myself.

In affirmation of this commitment, I will abide by the Code of Ethics of the Ministers Council of the American Baptist Churches and I will faithfully support its purposes and ideals. As further affirmation of my commitment, I covenant with my colleagues in ministry that we will hold one another accountable for fulfillment of all the public actions set forth in our Code of Ethics.

• I will hold in trust the traditions and practices of our American Baptist Churches; I will not accept a position in the American Baptist family unless I am in accord with those traditions and practices; nor will I use my influence to alienate my congregation/constituents or any part thereof from its relationship and support of the denomination. If my convictions change, I will resign my position.

• I will respect and recognize the variety of calls to ministry among my American Baptist colleagues, and other Christians.

• I will seek to support all colleagues in ministry by building constructive relationships wherever I serve, both with the staff where I work and with colleagues in neighboring churches.

• I will advocate adequate compensation for my profession. I will help lay persons and colleagues to understand that ministerial leaders should not expect or require fees for pastoral services from constituents they serve, when these constituents are helping pay their salaries.

• I will not seek personal favors or discounts on the basis of my professional status.

• I will maintain a disciplined ministry in such ways as keeping hours of prayers and devotion, endeavoring to maintain wholesome family relationships, sexual integrity, financial responsibility, regularly engaging in educational and recreational activities for professional and personal development. I will seek to maintain good health habits.

• I will recognize my primary obligation to the church or employing group to which I have been called, and will accept added responsibilities only if they do not interfere with the overall effectiveness of my ministry.

• I will personally and publicly support my colleagues who experience discrimination on the basis of gender, race, age, marital status, national origin, physical impairment, or disability.

• I will, upon my resignation or retirement, sever my ministerial leadership relations with my former constituents, and will not make professional contacts in the field of another ministerial leader without his/her request and/or consent.

• I will hold in confidence any privileged communication received by me during the conduct of my ministry. I will not disclose confidential communications in private or public except when in my practice of ministry I am convinced that the sanctity of confidentiality is outweighed by my well-founded belief that the parishioner/client will cause imminent, life-threatening, or substantial harm to self or others, or unless the privilege is waived by those giving the information.

• I will not proselytize from other Christian churches.

• I will show my personal love for God as revealed in Jesus Christ in my life and ministry, as I strive together with my colleagues to preserve the dignity, maintain the discipline, and promote the integrity of the vocation to which we have been called.

Signed _____

Date _____

(This code is available from www.ministerscouncil.com in English, French, Portuguese, and Spanish.)

Tracking Worship Components Usage

Date	Chorus/Hymns	Call to Worship	Scriptures	Sermon Title	Illustrations	Benediction

Service Components
for Child Dedication

Typical Order of Service to beadapted into a Handout with Parent(s)

Opening Remarks–Pastor

Sample opening remarks for the pastor (before the prayer)

- The dedication of a child, with their parents, is always a very significant and sacred occasion. It is that special time, when through sacred vows before God, the immediate family, and we as a church family, all commit ourselves to the raising of this child in the love and nurture of our faith.

- Dedication does not give a child salvation—that will be the child's individual choice as they grow up—but it confirms for all of us the intent of these parents, and ourselves as a church, to do all we can to cause these children, at an early age, to desire the faith and commitment that they see within us.

- Life is a precious gift from God. Thus it is fitting to begin this ceremony by giving God thanks for this precious, healthy new life.

- _____ will lead us in this prayer.

Prayer of Thanksgiving for the Gift of Life–the father, mother, other relative, or pastor

Sample For Prayer of Thanksgiving for the Gift of Life

Father God, we especially thank you for the precious gift of life. Thank you for granting this joy to _____ and _____. Thank you for helping them through the birthing process, for strengthening them through the painful parts, for answering their prayers for a healthy child (or for the gift of a child in cases where the child's health is in question). And thank you for family and friends, gathered here to celebrate this special and sacred occasion. Bless us together as we dedicate this child to you. In Jesus' name. Amen.

Dedication Prayer (Pastor holds infant or child for this part)
Sample Prayers of Dedication

Option 1: Thank you, gracious Father, for _____ & _____'s love for you and for one another. Thank you for blessing that love with _____ precious gifts of life. (List each child by name and then newborn). In these sacred moments, we dedicate _____ _____ back to you. We ask for your involvement in the life of this family in a dynamic way. Grant that early in his/her life, _____ might come to know you personally too, because of the example he/she sees around him/her. Help us, each one, to be supportive whenever _____ & _____ (parents, siblings, and newborn) need us. To this end we dedicate ourselves and these parents, with their child _____, to you our loving Father. Amen.

Option 2: Gracious God, we praise you for the life of _____ and _____, and for blessing their union with _____ _____. Thank you for _____ and _____'s willingness to voice these vows of commitment today, in dedicating their child to you. Grant them the needed strength and courage to indeed carry out these vows that they have made today, and grant by your grace, that early in life their son/daughter will come to understand and claim for himself/herself salvation by Jesus Christ. To this end we dedicate _____ to you our Lord, and ask that you might help each of us be supportive of (parents, child), whenever they need us. We praise you, Lord, for what you will do, in and through the precious lives of this family. Amen.

- Personal choice(s) (Medley of Scriptures also possible.)
- Suggestions:
Deuteronomy 6:1-9
1 Samuel 1:9-20
Psalm 127:1-5
Psalm 128:1-4
Psalm 139:1-18
Mark 10:13-16
- Involvement of Siblings?

Vows for the Parents

Pastor: _____ & _____, do you wish now to publicly present _____ to God in recognition of the high privilege and unique responsibility that God has granted to you as his/her parents?

Parents: We do.

Pastor: As _____ parents, do you recognize and solemnly declare your dependence upon Almighty God for the wisdom, help and blessing you will need to guide and nurture this child?

Parents: We do.

Pastor: Do you promise and commit yourselves to teach your child the truths and commitments of the Christian faith, and through purposeful prayer and personal example, seek to lead your child to personal faith in God through Jesus Christ?

Parents: We do.

Vows for Sibling(s)

Will you _____, as _____'s brother/sister, love _____ and help him/her learn to love Jesus?

Sibling(s): We/I will.

Vows for the Grandparents, Great Grandparents, or Godparents

92

Do you as grandparents/great grandparents/godparents (list by
name), commit yourselves to do your part, both through personal
example and loving support of these your adult children/dear
friends, as they seek to raise your grandchild/godchild in the love
and nurture of our faith?
Response: We do.

Vows for the Congregation

Pastor: As a congregation we have heard these parents and their
family/friends declare their desire to present _____ _____ to
God and to dedicate themselves to his/her Christian nurture. They
will also need us, as God's people, to support and assist them in
these efforts.

As a concrete way of showing your willingness to assume this
responsibility as their church family, to stand by them in their par-
enting, I invite you to stand with us now for the Dedication prayer.

Sample Pastoral Time Tracking Forms

Tracking What Hours Are Put In

1. At the end of each day, look at your appointment book and chart use of each 15-minute segment according to the categories in your job description. (This task is much easier if you keep a daily appointment calendar on your desk with lines for at least each half hour. Jot activities in as they are completed, to help keep track of time actually used for each task. Remember to include evenings worked.)

2. After a week of charting, combine the results under headings drawn from your job description, such as sermon preparation, visitation, administration, counseling, future planning, devotions, meetings attended, etc.

3. Do this for a week, even though it is very mundane. Then take a break and do another sample week later in the month. With this data the month can be estimated (or chart it for the whole month if you can stick with it). Present this information to your accountability group and evaluate together if this is the best use of your time.

4. Follow this same process as often as possible in a year, trying to pick the "more typical" weeks of pastoral work. This will make it possible to project a report for the year as well, which fits well in an annual report to the church.

Activities That Go into the Hours

On your weekly agenda, statistically keep tract of the following activities, then total them into a monthly report:

Activity	This Month	Year-To-Date
Worship Services Led		
Sermons Preached		
Lessons Taught		
Special Services		
Meetings Attended		
Hospital Visits		
Home Visits		
Pastoral care phone calls		
Correspondence sent		
Visitor letters		
Office visits		

The year-to-date feature is quite helpful in showing the big picture, including how many visitors have attended during the given year.